KFK KINGFISHER KNOWLEDGE

MICROSCOPIC LIFE

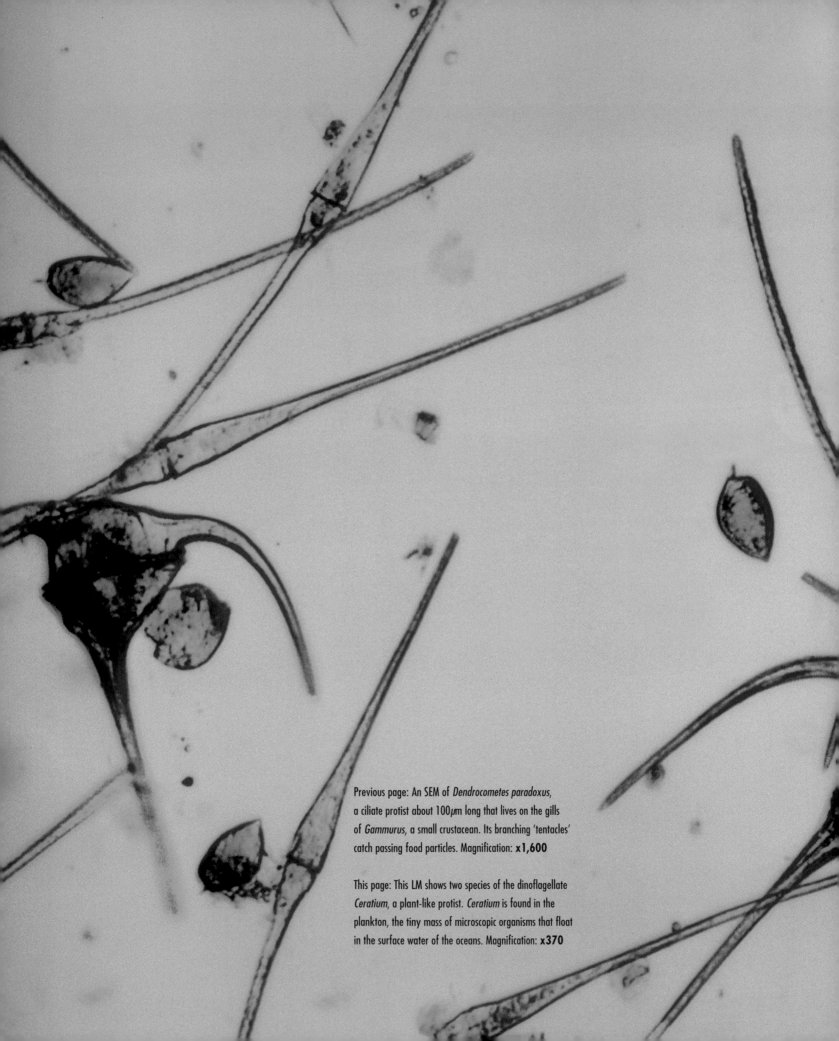

Previous page: An SEM of *Dendrocometes paradoxus*, a ciliate protist about 100μm long that lives on the gills of *Gammurus*, a small crustacean. Its branching 'tentacles' catch passing food particles. Magnification: **x1,600**

This page: This LM shows two species of the dinoflagellate *Ceratium*, a plant-like protist. *Ceratium* is found in the plankton, the tiny mass of microscopic organisms that float in the surface water of the oceans. Magnification: **x370**

MICROSCOPIC LIFE

Richard Walker

Foreword by
Professor Peter C Doherty

KINGFISHER

Senior editor: Carron Brown
Senior designer: Peter Clayman
Picture research: Rachael Swann
Consultant: Dr John Grainger, Chairman of MISAC (Microbiology
    in Schools Advisory Committee)
Production controller: Lindsey Scott
DTP co-ordinators: Sarah Pfitzner, Jonathan Pledge
Artwork archivists: Wendy Allison, Jenny Lord
Proofreader: Sheila Clewley

KINGFISHER
Kingfisher Publications Plc, New Penderel House,
283–288 High Holborn, London WC1V 7HZ
www.kingfisherpub.com

First published by Kingfisher Publications Plc 2004

10 9 8 7 6 5 4 3 2 1

1TR/0604/TWP/MA(MA)/130ENSOMA/F

ISBN 0 7534 0923 2

Printed in Singapore

Contents

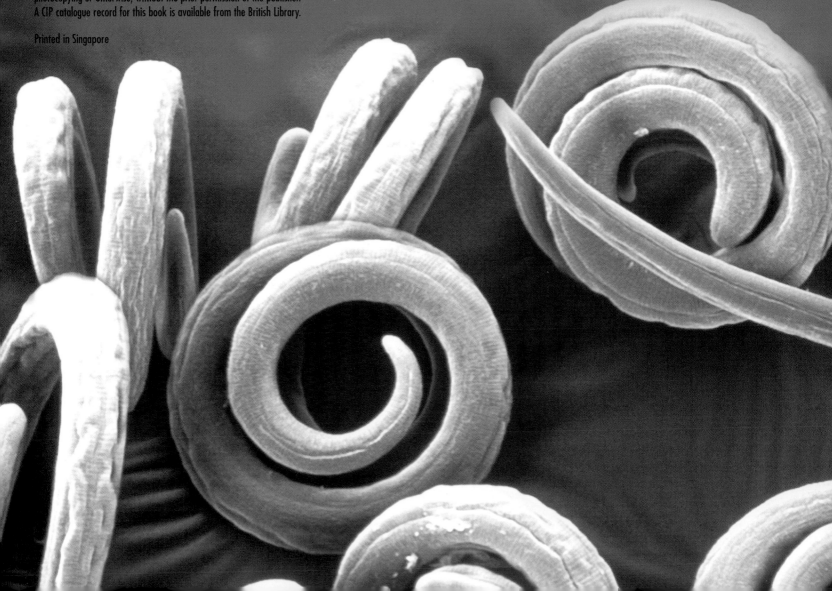

GO FURTHER...
INFORMATION PANEL KEY:

websites and further reading

career paths

places to visit

NOTE TO READERS (1)
The website addresses listed in this book are correct at the time of going to print. However, due to the ever-changing nature of the internet, website addresses and content can change. Websites can contain links that are unsuitable for children. The publisher cannot be held responsible for changes in website addresses or content, or for information obtained through third-party websites. We strongly advise that internet searches should be supervised by an adult.

NOTE TO READERS (2)
All measurements are abbreviated throughout this book. Please see pages 10–11 for an explanation of the measurements and their abbreviations.

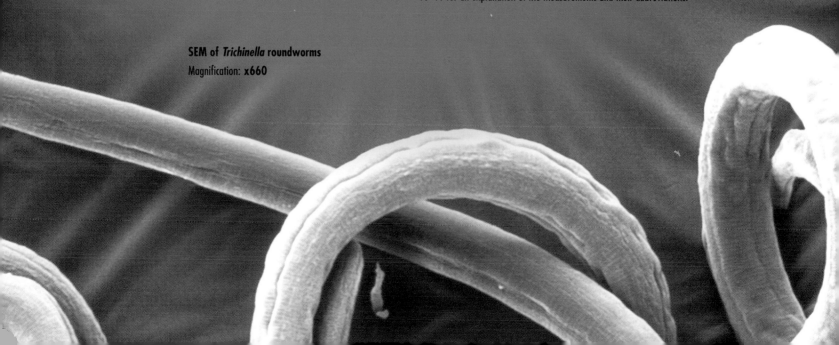

SEM of *Trichinella* roundworms
Magnification: x660

Foreword

My life as a research scientist has been spent trying to understand how the body deals with the invasion of simpler life forms, such as bacteria, fungi and viruses. We know what we can see. Before the microscope, before the Germ Theory of disease, people thought that infections were a property of 'miasmas' (toxic vapours), of malevolent acts by evil enemies, or resulted from the whim of the gods. In the plague years of the Middle Ages, minorities were killed for 'poisoning the wells' and isolated women were burned for the practice of witchcraft.

With Antony van Leeuwenhoek, humans saw for the first time the minutiae of life that surrounds us. Microscopy opened up the study of bacteriology. Robert Koch could stain and see the *tubercle* bacillus (the bacterium that causes tuberculosis) through the lens of his microscope. I recently purchased an elegant, brass instrument built in 1882 by the firm of Ernst Leitz in Wetzlar, Germany. The year 1882 came after Darwin's publication *On the Origin of Species*, but before Ronald Ross discovered the *plasmodium* protozoan that causes malaria. My antique Leitz monocular would have no trouble showing the malaria parasite. It could not, however, be used to see the influenza viruses or the human immunodeficiency virus (HIV) that is the focus of my current research programme. Such organisms can be visualized using the electron microscopes that, with the progress of technology, continue to advance our understanding.

My contemporary, 21st-century research group uses a diverse range of sophisticated instrumentation to analyze the characteristics of the virus-specific host response. This equipment ranges from flow cytometers that depend on laser and computer technology to characterize and separate the responding lymphocyte populations, to thermal cyclers that amplify molecular messages for analysis using genome technology. We use instruments that combine light microscopy and digital technology to measure the magnitude of cellular immunity. Most of our experiments begin with a young scientist or technician examining the cell populations with a conventional light microscope that is not so different from my 1882 veteran.

Modern science, and the progressive revolution it has brought to the human condition, has been in progress for about 500 years. Van Leeuwenhoek, whose simple microscopes can be seen today in the Boerhaave Museum in Leiden, Netherlands, lived from 1632–1723. The first of the great scientific academies, the Royal Society of London and the science section of the Academie Française, were founded in 1660 and 1663 respectively. The microscope has been with us from the earliest days of this enormous enterprise that has so illuminated the natural world for us and so changed the way that we live and think. The capacity to see is there for those who choose to look and to learn.

Professor Peter C Doherty – joint winner of the 1996 Nobel Prize for Physiology or Medicine, and Fellow of the Royal Society

SEM of tiny pollen grains from
flowers of the ragweed plant
Magnification: x3,250

CHAPTER 1

Microlife revealed

Imagine an object as small as the sharp point of a needle. Something so small we can only just see it. Now try to imagine something even smaller. Why? Because beyond our vision exists an amazing world populated by unimaginably huge numbers of tiny creatures called micro-organisms or microbes, hundreds or thousands of times smaller than that needle-tip. We know these creatures exist because microscopes magnify the tiniest life forms to make visible what was previously invisible. The study of micro-organisms is called microbiology. As well as micro-organisms, such as viruses and bacteria, microscopes also allow us to see in detail fungal spores, mini-animals and plant pollen. For 150 years, microbiologists have studied microbes to discover what they look like and how they live. Thanks to them, microlife has been revealed.

Unseen world

The world around us is teeming with tiny living things. Some are just visible to the naked eye, but many are so small they can be seen only with a microscope. These tiny living things include mini-animals and smaller forms called micro-organisms or microbes. There is an amazing variety of microbes and they are found virtually everywhere on earth. Here, you can see four creatures that live unseen in the microscopic world. Their size on this page is no guide to their size in real life – the mini-animal *Daphnia* is 150 times bigger than the microbe *Chlamydomonas*!

A world of variety

Inhabitants of the microworld include viruses, bacteria, protists, microscopic fungi and mini-animals. Chemical packages called viruses are the smallest of all microbes. Bacteria, such as *Streptococcus*, consist of single, simple cells. Protists consist of single cells and include algae, such as *Chlamydomonas*. Fungi are mostly multicellular and can be large such as mushrooms, or microscopic such as the soil fungus *Arthrobotrys*. Mini-animals are multicellular, and include minute crustaceans, such as *Daphnia*.

▶ This SEM shows *Streptococcus* bacteria taken from a person with a throat infection. The spherical-shaped bacteria, each between 0.7 and 1 μm long, are often joined together in a chain.

▲ A microbiology researcher investigates cells infected with a virus. The whole procedure takes place in a special cabinet with a screen separating the researcher from the cells. He is wearing a face mask, gloves and protective clothes to reduce the possibility of being infected by the virus.

Lifestyles

Micro-organisms follow many different lifestyles. Protists include those, like animals, that take in food, and those, like plants, that make food by photosynthesis. Some fungi are parasites, but many also gain nutrients from dead plants and animals. Bacteria include parasites such as *Streptococcus*, a pathogen (disease-causing microbe) that can live in humans and make them ill. But only one in 10,000 types of bacteria causes disease. Others live harmlessly on living things, and many more feed on dead or decaying material. All viruses are parasites, and most cause diseases because they invade living cells (of bacteria, animals or plants) to reproduce.

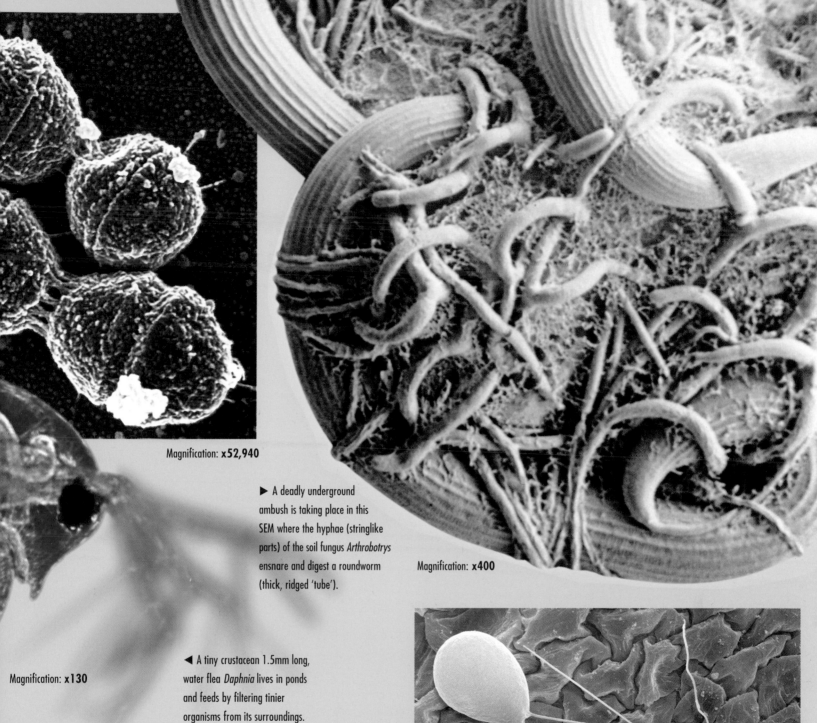

Magnification: **x52,940**

Magnification: **x130**

▶ A deadly underground ambush is taking place in this SEM where the hyphae (stringlike parts) of the soil fungus *Arthrobotrys* ensnare and digest a roundworm (thick, ridged 'tube').

Magnification: **x400**

◀ A tiny crustacean 1.5mm long, water flea *Daphnia* lives in ponds and feeds by filtering tinier organisms from its surroundings.

Habitats

Micro-organisms are everywhere. A microscopic snapshot of the back of your hand – or anywhere else on your skin – would reveal billions of bacteria. Look at soil, rocks, clouds, lakes, oceans, deserts, mountain tops, and bacteria will be there too. Other microbes are also widespread. Protists populate puddles, ponds, tree trunks and seas, not to mention blood vessels and intestines. Tiny fungal spores float through the air and grow wherever suitable food is to be found. And there are so many tiny soil roundworms that if all the earth's soil was to be blown away, the shape of continents would be preserved by their bodies!

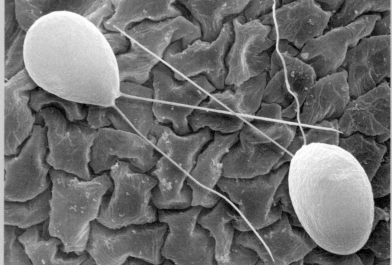

▲ This SEM shows two pear-shaped green algae called *Chlamydomonas*, which live in fresh water and move rapidly by beating the two whiplash flagella at their front end. Each is about 10μm long (not including flagella). *Chlamydomonas* uses sunlight energy to make its own food. Magnification: **x2,950**

Size and scale

Because they cannot be seen with the naked eye, it can be difficult to understand how small microbes really are, or how small the smallest is compared to the biggest. This is made more confusing because micrographs enlarge microscopic organisms by different amounts, so the tiniest can look bigger than the largest. In this book, measurement and magnification are clearly shown, as explained below.

▶ A dust mite (see page 31) rests on the tip of a sewing needle. Magnification makes it look 130mm long. In reality, it is just 0.3mm long. The magnified mite is 130 ÷ 0.3 = 433 times bigger than life size.

100nm (0.1μm or 0.0001mm)

▲ VIRUS – Magnification: **x500,000**
Viruses are the smallest microbes and most are between 10 and 100nm in size. This flu virus (see page 22) is 85nm across.

1μm (0.001mm)

▲ BACTERIUM – Magnification: **x50,000**
This sore throat-causing *Streptococcus* bacterium (see pages 8–9) is about 1μm long. Most bacteria are between 1 and 4μm long.

10μm (0.01mm)

▲ PROTIST – Magnification: **x5,000**
This trypanosome protist (see pages 48–49) is about 10μm long, 10 times bigger than *Streptococcus*. Most protists are 10 to 200μm long.

Measuring micro-organisms

Throughout this book the size of micro-organisms is given in metric units, the system of measurement used by all scientists around the world. Measurement of length (see table on the opposite page) is based on the metre (m), although this is too big to be useful here. Few of the organisms in the book are longer than one millimetre (mm) – a thousand times smaller than one metre, and the width of the letter 'i' in the word 'Size' in the heading at the top of this page. Most microbes are much smaller and are measured in micrometres (μm), or thousandths of a millimetre. Viruses are very small and so are measured in nanometres (nm), or millionths of a millimetre.

Scale and magnification

All the micro-organisms in this book are shown larger-than-life. We use scale and magnification to understand how an organism's size on a page relates to its real size. The six squares above show how this works. In the first square (top left), 50mm (the width of the square) represents 100nm (0.0001mm) in real size. That is a scale of 50:0.0001 or 500,000:1. So the virus in the square has been magnified, or enlarged, 500,000 times (x500,000). In the second square, 50mm represents 1μm, a scale of 50,000:1, magnifying the bacterium 50,000 times. So in real life the bacterium is about 10 times bigger than the virus. Similarly, the next square represents an organism 10 times bigger, and so on.

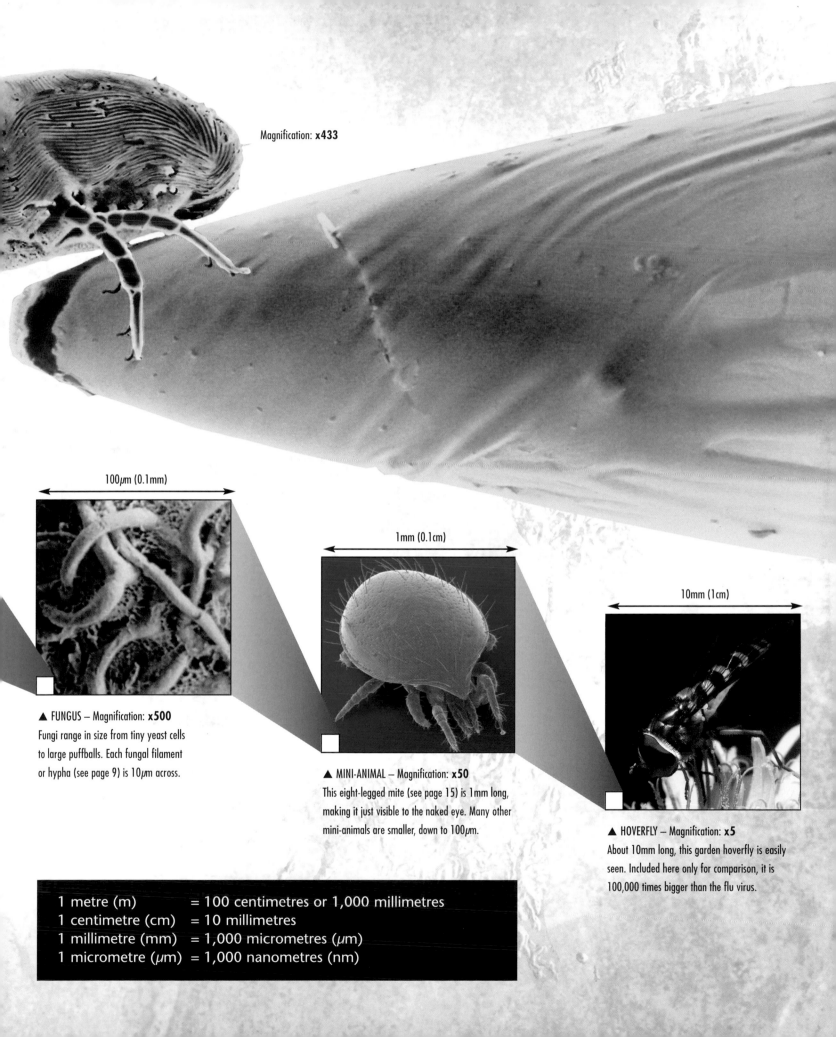

Magnification: **x433**

100μm (0.1mm)

▲ FUNGUS – Magnification: **x500**
Fungi range in size from tiny yeast cells
to large puffballs. Each fungal filament
or hypha (see page 9) is 10μm across.

1mm (0.1cm)

▲ MINI-ANIMAL – Magnification: **x50**
This eight-legged mite (see page 15) is 1mm long,
making it just visible to the naked eye. Many other
mini-animals are smaller, down to 100μm.

10mm (1cm)

▲ HOVERFLY – Magnification: **x5**
About 10mm long, this garden hoverfly is easily
seen. Included here only for comparison, it is
100,000 times bigger than the flu virus.

1 metre (m)	= 100 centimetres or 1,000 millimetres
1 centimetre (cm)	= 10 millimetres
1 millimetre (mm)	= 1,000 micrometres (μm)
1 micrometre (μm)	= 1,000 nanometres (nm)

single lens

object placed
on a pin

◄ Van Leeuwenhoek's microscope
consisted of a single convex lens
clamped between two brass plates.
It was held as shown and the
flat side was brought up close
to the eye. The specimen, placed
on a pin, was then viewed through
the lens against a source of
light such as a candle.

Under the microscope

At the end of the 16th century, a remarkable invention changed the study of organisms forever. Hans and Zacharias Janssen, a father-and-son team of spectacle makers in Holland, constructed an instrument (later to be called the compound microscope) that used two glass lenses to magnify tiny objects. In the 17th century, Antony van Leeuwenhoek and Robert Hooke used microscopes to reveal a world previously hidden from human sight. That world is populated by tiny organisms that are less than 0.2mm (200μm) across, too small to be seen with the naked eye.

Van Leeuwenhoek's animalcules

Dutch cloth merchant Antony van Leeuwenhoek (1632–1723) made his own simple microscope using only one small convex lens that could magnify up to 300 times. By examining samples taken from soil, puddles and other sources, he became the first person ever to see micro-organisms, which he called 'animalcules' or 'tiny animals'. Van Leeuwenhoek made detailed drawings and between 1674–1676 established his reputation by reporting his findings to the Royal Society of London. In 1683, he saw numerous tiny organisms in scrapings from his teeth, the first time that bacteria had ever been seen. As van Leeuwenhoek noted: 'There are more animalcules in the scum on the teeth in a man's mouth than there are men in a whole kingdom'.

Hooke's discoveries

English scientist Robert Hooke (1635–1703) built his own compound microscope, which could achieve magnifications of x300 and x500, although the images were blurred at the edges. Despite this, Hooke used his excellent drawing skills to record his findings in the book *Micrographia*, published by the Royal Society in 1665. One drawing showed a thin slice of cork containing many tiny 'chambers'. Hooke called them 'cells', the word we now use to describe the building blocks of life (see pages 18–19).

Compound microscopes

Compound microscopes today are also called light microscopes because they use light to illuminate organisms. Light passing though a specimen is magnified by the microscope's objective (lower) lens, and then again by the eyepiece (upper) lens before being seen as an enlarged image. Light microscopes usually magnify up to x1,000. A photograph taken using a light microscope is called a light micrograph (LM).

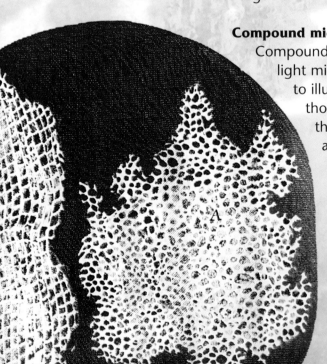

◄ This drawing of a section through cork, taken from Robert Hooke's *Micrographia*, shows the tiny chambers he called 'cells'.

Contrast and staining

Most micro-organisms are transparent, and so are invisible to us even when magnified. Contrast makes an organism, or its parts, visible by making it stand out from its surroundings. An easy way to do this is to use chemicals called stains that add colour to organisms, as shown in the picture below. However, most stains can be used only when organisms are dead, and so they cannot be seen moving. One way to see living organisms is to use different forms of lighting to obtain contrast, such as showing the specimen as a bright object on a dark background (see the LM of *Vorticella* on page 18).

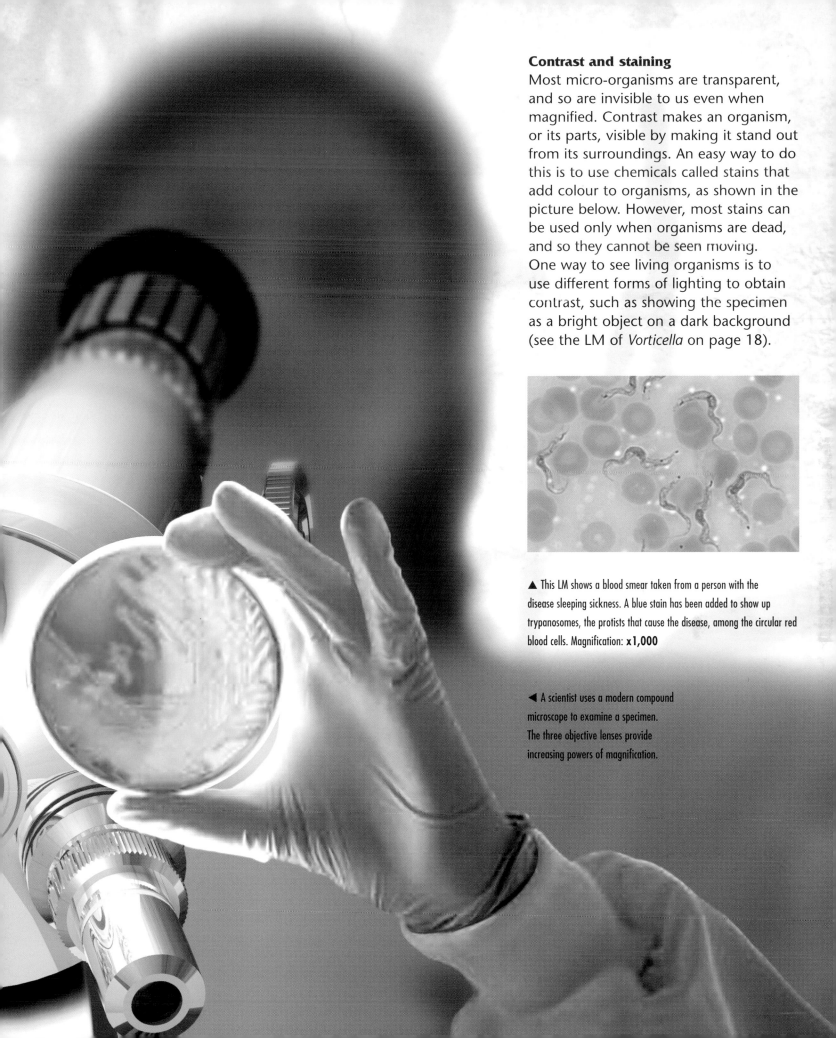

▲ This LM shows a blood smear taken from a person with the disease sleeping sickness. A blue stain has been added to show up trypanosomes, the protists that cause the disease, among the circular red blood cells. Magnification: **x1,000**

◀ A scientist uses a modern compound microscope to examine a specimen. The three objective lenses provide increasing powers of magnification.

Smaller and smaller

Invented in the 1930s, powerful electron microscopes can magnify tiny objects much more than any light microscope. Electron microscopes have transformed our understanding of microscopic life by allowing scientists to explore in great detail the structure of tiny organisms, and to see for the first time very small objects such as viruses. The four micrographs shown here were produced using either transmission or scanning electron microscopes. In each case, false colours have been added to the otherwise black-and-white image.

Transmission electron microscopes

Imagine sitting in the dark and shining a torch through your fingers. When the torch beam hits your hand, the light is scattered by your fingers and the shadow image of your hand is projected onto a wall. Transmission electron microscopes work in a similar way, but use tiny particles called electrons instead of light. An electron 'gun' at the top of the tube-like microscope fires a fast-moving beam of electrons through a thin slice of the specimen. Some parts of the specimen scatter electrons, just as your fingers scatter the torch beam. The beam of scattered electrons is then focused by magnets onto a TV screen to reveal a magnified view of the specimen. This image can be 'captured' as a transmission electron micrograph (TEM).

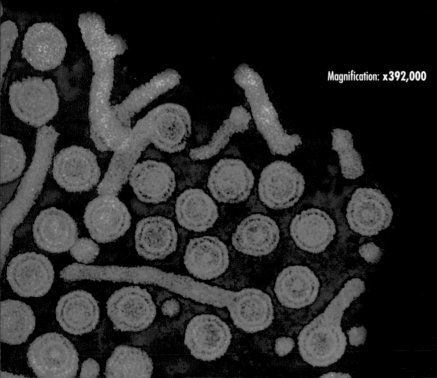

Magnification: **x392,000**

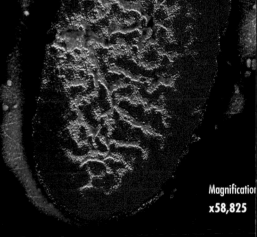

▶ This TEM shows a section through a bacterium called *Bordetella pertussis*. Around 1.4μm long, it causes the disease whooping cough, or pertussis.

◀ A cross-section of the virus that causes hepatitis, a liver disease, is shown in this TEM. Each virus particle (a blue circle) is just 30nm across.

Magnification
x58,825

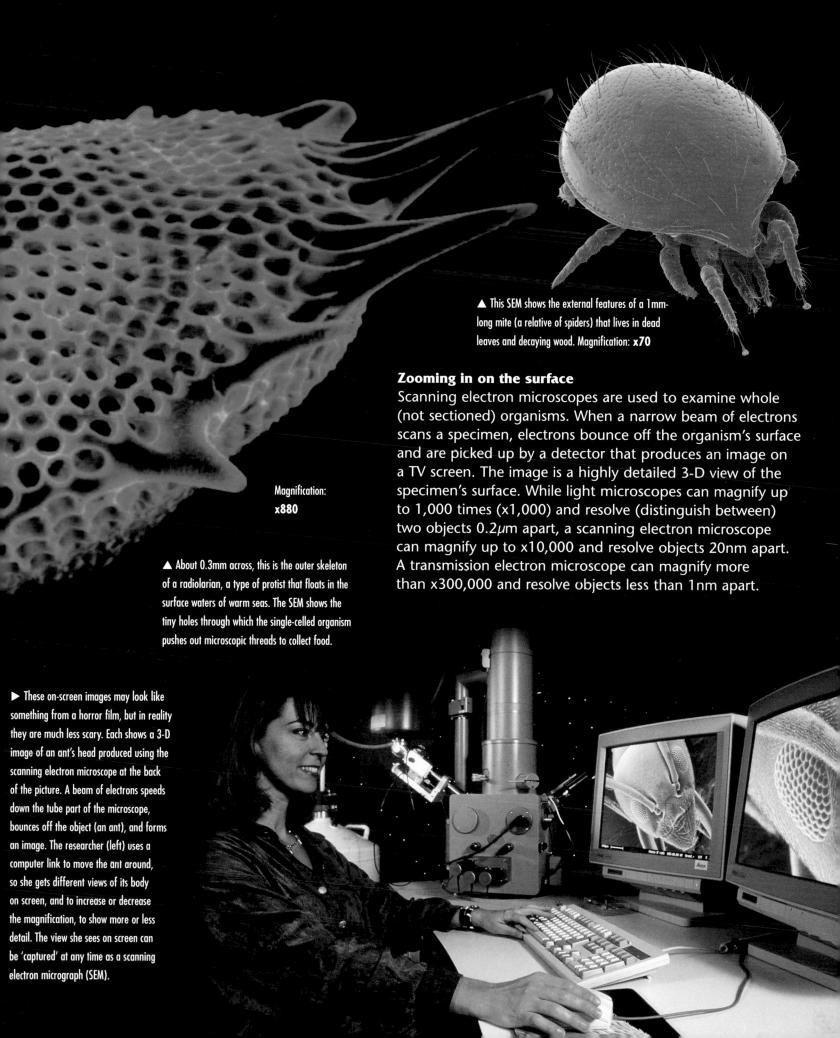

▲ This SEM shows the external features of a 1mm-long mite (a relative of spiders) that lives in dead leaves and decaying wood. Magnification: **x70**

Zooming in on the surface

Scanning electron microscopes are used to examine whole (not sectioned) organisms. When a narrow beam of electrons scans a specimen, electrons bounce off the organism's surface and are picked up by a detector that produces an image on a TV screen. The image is a highly detailed 3-D view of the specimen's surface. While light microscopes can magnify up to 1,000 times (x1,000) and resolve (distinguish between) two objects $0.2\mu m$ apart, a scanning electron microscope can magnify up to x10,000 and resolve objects 20nm apart. A transmission electron microscope can magnify more than x300,000 and resolve objects less than 1nm apart.

Magnification:
x880

▲ About 0.3mm across, this is the outer skeleton of a radiolarian, a type of protist that floats in the surface waters of warm seas. The SEM shows the tiny holes through which the single-celled organism pushes out microscopic threads to collect food.

▶ These on-screen images may look like something from a horror film, but in reality they are much less scary. Each shows a 3-D image of an ant's head produced using the scanning electron microscope at the back of the picture. A beam of electrons speeds down the tube part of the microscope, bounces off the object (an ant), and forms an image. The researcher (left) uses a computer link to move the ant around, so she gets different views of its body on screen, and to increase or decrease the magnification, to show more or less detail. The view she sees on screen can be 'captured' at any time as a scanning electron micrograph (SEM).

Life from nowhere?

From the time of the ancient Greeks, around 2,400 years ago, right up until the 19th century, there was a widespread belief that living organisms could arise from non-living or decaying matter. This sudden appearance of life from nowhere was called spontaneous generation. The discovery of micro-organisms in the 17th century made spontaneous generation seem even more possible. It took the work of a brilliant French scientist to finally disprove the idea.

Spontaneous generation

Greek philosopher Aristotle (384–322 BCE), thought the idea that small animals, such as worms, arose spontaneously from mud was simply common sense. This belief was passed down over the centuries. Nearly 2,000 years after Aristotle, Belgian scientist Johannes van Helmont (1579–1644) left wheat grains wrapped in sweaty shirts in an open barrel. When, after 21 days, mice were found there, van Helmont concluded that they had arisen spontaneously from the sweat and wheat. He had 'proved' spontaneous generation existed!

Maggots from meat

Another common belief was that maggots arose spontaneously from rotting meat. In 1668, Italian physician Francesco Redi (1626–97) tested this idea. He placed meat in two containers – one open to the air and one covered with gauze that allowed air into the container, but not flies. The meat in the open was soon covered by maggots. The covered meat remained maggot-free because flies could not reach the meat to lay their eggs. Redi's experiment disproved the spontaneous generation of maggots.

▲ Maggots (fly larvae) feeding on meat do not arise spontaneously.
They hatch from eggs laid by female flies. Magnification: **x3**

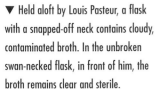

▼ Held aloft by Louis Pasteur, a flask with a snapped-off neck contains cloudy, contaminated broth. In the unbroken swan-necked flask, in front of him, the broth remains clear and sterile.

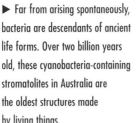

▶ Far from arising spontaneously, bacteria are descendants of ancient life forms. Over two billion years old, these cyanobacteria-containing stromatolites in Australia are the oldest structures made by living things.

Pasteur's proof

Despite Redi's work, people still believed that microbes could arise spontaneously. But in 1859, microbiologist Louis Pasteur (1822–95) settled the matter. He placed clear broth in a flask and heated the flask's neck to draw it out into a curve shaped like a swan's neck. He then boiled the broth to sterilize it (make it microbe-free). Once cool, it stayed sterile and clear though it was exposed to the air – any microbes from the air had been trapped in the curved neck. When he snapped off the neck, microbes got into the broth and made it cloudy as they multiplied. Pasteur had proved that life arises only from pre-existing life.

The building blocks of life

Every organism on earth, from the smallest bacterium to the mightiest whale, is made up of tiny living units called cells. Some organisms, such as protists, consist of just one cell. Others are made from thousands, millions or billions of cells. Using microscopes, scientists have shown that while the cells of protists, fungi, plants and animals – known as eukaryotic cells – vary in shape and size, they share many common features. Bacterial cells, known as prokaryotic cells, also share some of these features, but have a simpler structure (see pages 24–25).

▲ An artist's view inside the alga *Chlamydomonas* shows that it contains a chloroplast (green) as well as standard cell components. It is moved by two whip-like flagella. Magnification: **x5,500**

Inside a eukaryotic cell

Before the invention of the electron microscope, cells were known to have only an outer boundary (plasma membrane) surrounding a control centre (nucleus) and, between the two, a jelly-like cytoplasm. Powerful electron microscopes then showed that the cytoplasm is more than a simple liquid, and also contains tiny structures called organelles ('little organs') such as mitochondria (singular – mitochondrion) that release energy from sugars by a process called cell respiration. This process powers all the chemical reactions taking place that make the cell alive. The folded membranes of the endoplasmic reticulum transport cell-building proteins made by the speck-like ribosomes. The nucleus holds DNA, the genetic material that contains the instructions needed to construct and operate the cell.

▶ This section through a 'typical' animal cell shows features that are found in all eukaryotic cells.

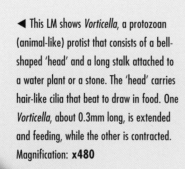

◀ This LM shows *Vorticella*, a protozoan (animal-like) protist that consists of a bell-shaped 'head' and a long stalk attached to a water plant or a stone. The 'head' carries hair-like cilia that beat to draw in food. One *Vorticella*, about 0.3mm long, is extended and feeding, while the other is contracted. Magnification: **x480**

Single cells

Most eukaryotic, unicellular (single-celled) micro-organisms belong to the protists, the group that includes algae and protozoa. Algae, such as *Chlamydomonas*, make their food by photosynthesis. In addition to standard eukaryotic cell parts, *Chlamydomonas* has a green chloroplast packed with light-trapping chlorophyll. Protozoa, such as *Vorticella*, either capture food or absorb it from their surroundings. Fixed in place, *Vorticella* has hair-like cilia that beat to create a current to draw in food. Its more mobile relatives use cilia to move. Other protozoa have long flagella to push or pull them through water. Other unicellular microbes include yeasts – microscopic fungi that absorb food from their surroundings.

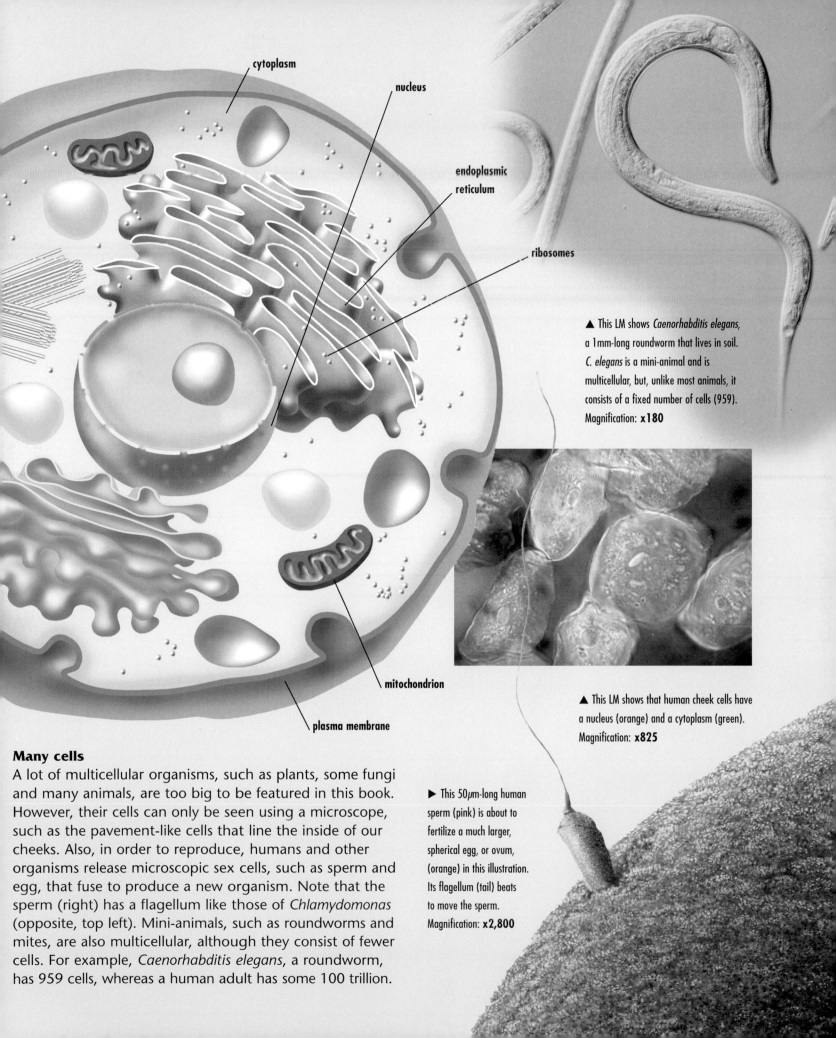

cytoplasm

nucleus

endoplasmic
reticulum

ribosomes

mitochondrion

plasma membrane

▲ This LM shows *Caenorhabditis elegans*, a 1mm-long roundworm that lives in soil. *C. elegans* is a mini-animal and is multicellular, but, unlike most animals, it consists of a fixed number of cells (959). Magnification: **x180**

▲ This LM shows that human cheek cells have a nucleus (orange) and a cytoplasm (green). Magnification: **x825**

▶ This 50μm-long human sperm (pink) is about to fertilize a much larger, spherical egg, or ovum, (orange) in this illustration. Its flagellum (tail) beats to move the sperm. Magnification: **x2,800**

Many cells

A lot of multicellular organisms, such as plants, some fungi and many animals, are too big to be featured in this book. However, their cells can only be seen using a microscope, such as the pavement-like cells that line the inside of our cheeks. Also, in order to reproduce, humans and other organisms release microscopic sex cells, such as sperm and egg, that fuse to produce a new organism. Note that the sperm (right) has a flagellum like those of *Chlamydomonas* (opposite, top left). Mini-animals, such as roundworms and mites, are also multicellular, although they consist of fewer cells. For example, *Caenorhabditis elegans*, a roundworm, has 959 cells, whereas a human adult has some 100 trillion.

SUMMARY OF CHAPTER 1: MICROLIFE REVEALED

An SEM of *Phthiracarus* – a soil mite that lives unseen in leaf-litter. A relative of spiders, this mini-animal also has eight legs. It helps to recycle nutrients by feeding on dead plant material.
Magnification: **x75**

Introducing the microworld

Unseen but all around us is a hidden world of microscopic organisms. They range in size and variety from millionths-of-a-millimetre-long viruses through bacteria, protists and microscopic fungi to mini-animals, such as water fleas, that are just visible to the naked eye. We can readily appreciate the difference in size between a mouse and an elephant. But the 'invisibility' of microlife makes it difficult for us to understand how small they are, or even how a water flea, say, is 15,000 times bigger than a virus. Here, we have seen how the millimetre (mm), micrometre (μm) and nanometre (nm) are used to measure and show differences in size between microbes. And how magnification makes a microscopic organism appear bigger so that, for example, being magnified 100 times (x100) means that the object is 100 times bigger than in real life.

Making things bigger

Invented just 400 years ago, microscopes changed our view of life by bringing the microworld into view for the first time. The first microscopes used light to illuminate minute specimens, and their more sophisticated descendants are still used today. But more powerful electron microscopes, invented in the 20th century, allow us to look deeper into the microworld by magnifying microscopic organisms much more, and by allowing us to see tiny creatures in far greater detail. Microscopes (both light and electron) have also enabled scientists to find out how cells – the basic units of all life, including micro-organisms – are built, how they function and how they always arise from other cells.

Go further...

Visit an interactive website about microbes at:
www.amnh.org/nationalcenter/infection

Find more about microbes at:
www.microbeworld.org

Compare the sizes of microbes at:
www.cellsalive.com/howbig.htm

For more about Robert Hooke and Antony van Leeuwenhoek, visit:
www.ucmp.berkeley.edu/history/hooke.html
and
www.ucmp.berkeley.edu/history/leeuwenhoek.html

See some amazing micrographs at:
www.denniskunkel.com/

Biochemist
Studies the chemical reactions that take place inside cells, including those of micro-organisms.

Cell biologist
Studies cells, their structure and how they work.

Microbiologist
Biologist who specializes in the study of micro-organisms, especially bacteria and viruses.

Microscopist
Using light and/or electron microscopes, examines and photographs cells and micro-organisms.

Visit the Musée Pasteur in the building where Pasteur carried out his experiments:
25 rue du Docteur Roux, 75015 Paris, France
Telephone: +33 (0) 1 45 68 82 83
www.pasteur.fr/pasteur/musees

See some of van Leeuwenhoek's microscopes at: Museum Boerhaave, Lange Sint, Agnietenstraat 10, 2313 WC, Leiden, Netherlands
Telephone: +31 (0) 71 5214224
www.museumboerhaave.nl

Hooke's microscope and many others are on display at: The Science Museum, Exhibition Road, South Kensington, London, SW7 2DD, UK
Telephone: +44 (0) 870 870 4868
www.sciencemuseum.org.uk

CHAPTER 2

Microscopic organisms

There are trillions and trillions of microscopic organisms – so many that despite each microbe being so small, together they far outweigh the planet's bigger life forms by over ten times. What is more, they are found everywhere, from high up in the atmosphere to the dark depths of the ocean, not to mention inside our noses, on our food and lurking in our beds. To make sense of this teeming mass of microscopic creatures, we classify, or collect them, into groups according to their shape, structure, size, lifestyle and how they are related to each other. These groups are viruses, bacteria, protists, tiny fungi and mini-animals.

This SEM shows *Hydra*, a freshwater mini-animal, anchored by its base to some pondweed. Its pink colour is completely artificial. It has been added to an otherwise black-and-white micrograph to provide contrast so that the *Hydra's* parts can be seen clearly. Magnification: x100

Magnification:
x675,000

virus envelope
with protein
spikes

protein coat
(capsid)

nucleic acid
(RNA)

Viruses

Of all microbes, viruses are the smallest and strangest. These non-living chemical packages neither feed nor grow, and become active only when they invade living cells, called hosts, in order to reproduce. Many viruses cause diseases in animals and plants. Viruses range in size from 25 to 300nm.

▲ This computer artwork shows the structure of a flu (influenza) virus, 85nm across. It has an outer protein coat, studded with spikes, and a core of nucleic acid (in this case RNA).

▼ A T4 bacteriophage virus (red), 250nm in height, injects its DNA through the cell wall (green) of an *E. coli* bacterium in this TEM. This virus has a complex shape with a regular 'head', a 'tail' and six 'legs'.

Magnification:
x350,000

Chemical packages

Every virus is packaged from a handful of chemical components. The core is made of a strand or strands of nucleic acid – either DNA or RNA – that carry the instructions to make more viruses. Surrounding this core is a protective protein coat called a capsid. This has spikes that enable the virus to attach itself to the surface of a host cell. Capsids vary greatly in shape. Some have regular shapes with straight sides while others are less regular. Viruses can invade all types of cells, including those of animals, plants, fungi, protists and bacteria. Bacteria-invading viruses are called bacteriophages. Unable to move on their own, viruses can be transferred from host to host in droplets in the air, in water or food, in infected blood, or by blood-sucking or plant-biting insects.

▼ This SEM shows an aphid using its piercing mouthparts to penetrate leaf cells to feed on sugary sap. These insects carry viruses and spread them between plants during feeding. Magnification: **x65**

▶ This diagram shows how a virus reproduces, using a bacteriophage and its *E. coli* host as an example:
1) Virus attaches to the bacterium
2) Virus tail injects DNA into bacterium
3) Virus DNA and proteins made inside bacterium
4) Newly assembled viruses emerge from bacterium.

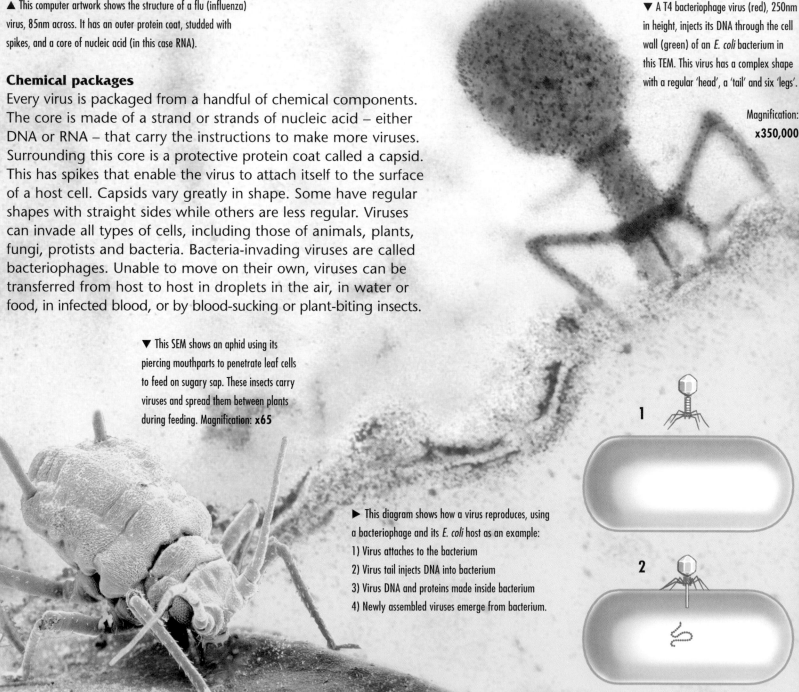

1

2

► This computer-generated image shows SARS (severe acute respiratory syndrome) viruses travelling through the air in water droplets as they pass from an infected person to be breathed in by an uninfected person. Clearly visible are the capsid (green) and its spikes (red). First identified in 2003, the virus causes a severe and sometimes fatal disease. It belongs to the coronaviruses, the group that usually causes mild or moderate respiratory (breathing) infections, such as colds, in humans. Magnification: **x600,000**

Virus reproduction

All viruses share the same life cycle, one that is totally different from any living organism. The illustration (below left) shows reproduction of a bacteriophage, but the same principles apply to other viruses. First the virus locks onto its target cell, then penetrates the cell and releases its DNA or RNA load. Once the DNA or RNA instructions have penetrated the host cell, they hijack its chemical machinery so it switches to producing multiple copies of the virus's nucleic acid core and protein coat. Once these components are made they are assembled into new virus particles. No longer required, the host cell bursts open to release the virus copies that go on to infect other cells and copy themselves once again.

Changing identity

Our body's immune system usually remembers a virus's identity so it does not infect us again. But some viruses, such as the flu virus, can change their identity and infect us repeatedly. Also, altering its identity can allow a virus to 'jump' from animals to humans. This is what happened in 2003 when the disease SARS appeared in Asia. The virus, normally found in cat-like civets, had changed and was able to infect human cells. Spread by coughs and sneezes, the new disease caused severe breathing problems. Around 8,000 cases and 750 deaths occurred world-wide, as SARS spread from Asia, before it was brought under control.

▼ A Chinese woman wears a face mask to help protect her from infection by SARS. The SARS virus, like common cold viruses, is carried through the air in tiny water droplets. The mask absorbs droplets, and stops the woman from breathing in virus particles.

3
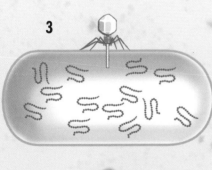

4
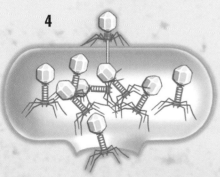

Bacteria

The smallest and most abundant of all living things, bacteria are everywhere – on land, in water, in the air, even on and in other living things. Each bacterium consists of a single, simple cell, and most live in groups or colonies within which they usually reproduce rapidly. Bacteria are often feared for the diseases they cause, such as food poisoning. But many bacteria benefit us by helping to produce the conditions that enable life on earth to exist.

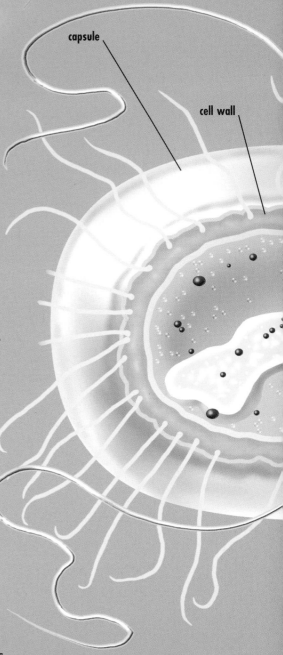

capsule

cell wall

▲ Bacteria not only live in clouds (background), they also grow and multiply there, as Austrian scientists discovered in 2000. Incredibly these bacteria, which originate from plants or soil on the earth's surface, may also influence climate by affecting cloud formation and rainfall.

Bacterial cells

Bacteria are prokaryotic cells, simpler in structure than the complex eukaryotic cells (see pages 18–19). Like eukaryotic cells, bacteria have a cytoplasm, a plasma membrane and ribosomes that make the cell's proteins, but they lack a nucleus. Instead, they have a nucleoid, a single loop of DNA containing the instructions needed to make and run the cell. Bacteria are shaped by a rigid cell wall, and some have a slimy outer jacket (the capsule) that protects it. Short 'hairs' called pili attach the bacterium to its food, and many also have longer flagella that beat and move the bacterium.

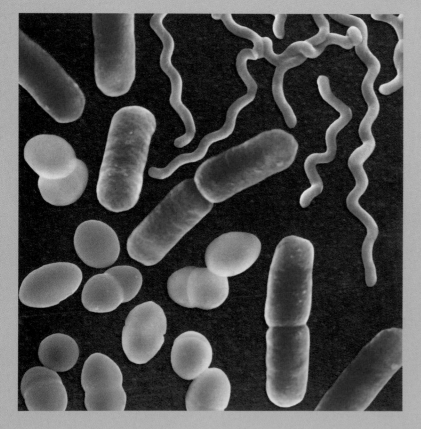

◄ This SEM compares the shapes of the three main types of bacteria. These are spherical bacteria or cocci (purple), rod-shaped bacteria or bacilli (pink), and spiral-shaped bacteria (blue). Magnification: **x10,000**

Sizes and shapes

Most bacteria are between 1μm and 4μm long – only visible in detail using an electron microscope. About 10,000 species of bacteria are known, although there are certainly many, many more. They can be divided into three groups – cocci, bacilli and spiral bacteria – according to their shape. Cocci (singular – coccus) are round and may occur singly, in pairs, in clumps or in chains, as in *Streptococcus* (see page 8). Bacilli (singular – bacillus) are straight, rod-shaped bacteria that include *Escherichia coli*. Spiral-shaped bacteria include corkscrew-like forms called spirochaetes, and comma-shaped cells called vibrios.

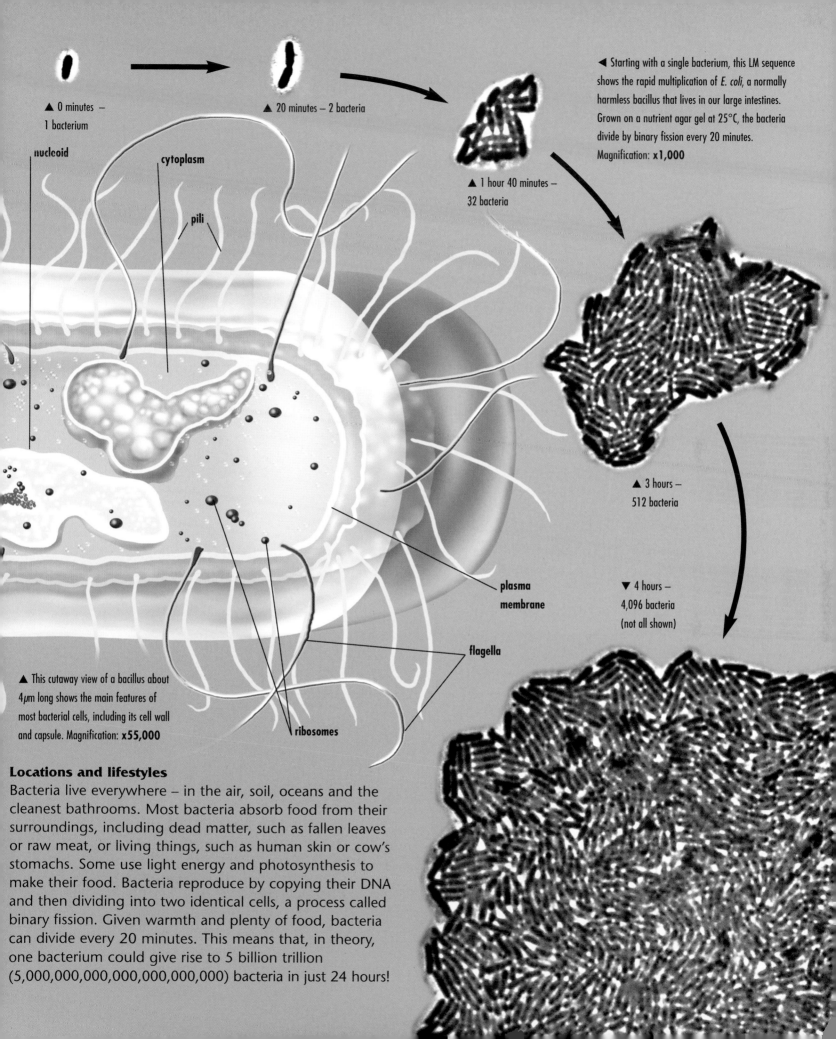

▲ 0 minutes –
1 bacterium

▲ 20 minutes – 2 bacteria

◄ Starting with a single bacterium, this LM sequence shows the rapid multiplication of *E. coli*, a normally harmless bacillus that lives in our large intestines. Grown on a nutrient agar gel at 25°C, the bacteria divide by binary fission every 20 minutes. Magnification: **x1,000**

▲ 1 hour 40 minutes –
32 bacteria

nucleoid

cytoplasm

pili

plasma
membrane

▲ 3 hours –
512 bacteria

▼ 4 hours –
4,096 bacteria
(not all shown)

flagella

▲ This cutaway view of a bacillus about 4μm long shows the main features of most bacterial cells, including its cell wall and capsule. Magnification: **x55,000**

ribosomes

Locations and lifestyles

Bacteria live everywhere – in the air, soil, oceans and the cleanest bathrooms. Most bacteria absorb food from their surroundings, including dead matter, such as fallen leaves or raw meat, or living things, such as human skin or cow's stomachs. Some use light energy and photosynthesis to make their food. Bacteria reproduce by copying their DNA and then dividing into two identical cells, a process called binary fission. Given warmth and plenty of food, bacteria can divide every 20 minutes. This means that, in theory, one bacterium could give rise to 5 billion trillion (5,000,000,000,000,000,000,000) bacteria in just 24 hours!

Protists

Found mainly in oceans and freshwater, as well as damp places on land, protists are single-celled organisms that show an incredible variety of forms including sun-like heliozoans, sculptured diatoms and amoebas that constantly change shape. Protist cells are eukaryotic and have their DNA enclosed inside a nucleus. Protists are usually divided into two main groups – the protozoa and the algae.

Magnification:
x875

Protozoa

Protozoa track down and gather food in the form of bacteria, other protists or particles of dead matter. They can be grouped as flagellates, amoeboids or ciliates, according to how they move. Flagellates have one or two long, whip-like flagella that beat to pull or push them through water. Amoeboids change shape, pushing out temporary pseudopodia ('false feet') to pull themselves along a solid surface. Some amoeboids have shells with holes through which they stick out their pseudopodia, while others, such as amoebas, are 'naked'. Ciliates have many small, hair-like projections called cilia that beat rhythmically, enabling them to move, turn or stop rapidly.

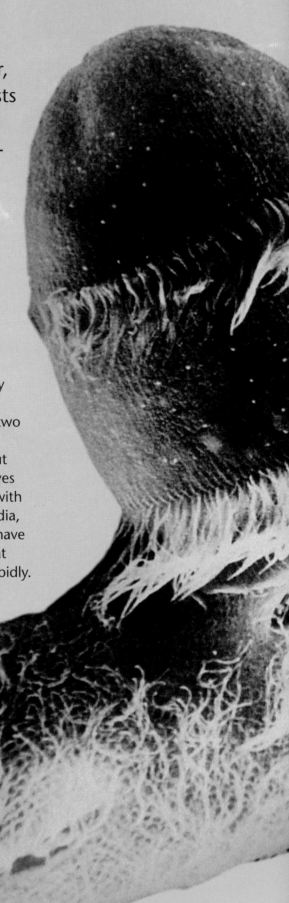

◄ This SEM shows *Euglena*, a green freshwater flagellate found in ponds and puddles, that usually makes its own food by photosynthesis. The long flagellum at its front end pulls *Euglena* through the water.

Algae

These plant-like protists use sunlight energy and photosynthesis to make their food. Algae include green algae, diatoms, dinoflagellates and euglenas. Many live in the surface waters of oceans and lakes where sunlight can penetrate, some moving with the water and others moving using their flagella. Together, this mass of floating algae forms phytoplankton (see pages 54–55), vitally important because of the life-giving oxygen it releases. Algae are also found in soil, and on rocks and tree trunks, as well as forming green slime in ponds and puddles. Some algae, such as *Euglena*, can also feed on other protists.

Protozoan lifestyles

The dramatic image below shows the predatory ciliate *Didinium* about to engulf its prey. As with many protozoa, once the prey is 'swallowed', it is enclosed inside the cell in a 'bag' called a food vacuole and digested. This is true of most protozoa that live freely in seas, lakes, ponds and in the soil. But a few protozoa are parasites that absorb food directly from their hosts (see pages 48–49). These parasites include the pathogenic protists that cause sleeping sickness, malaria and, in the case of *Entamoeba*, dysentery. Whether they are parasites or free-living, most protozoa reproduce by dividing in two (binary fission).

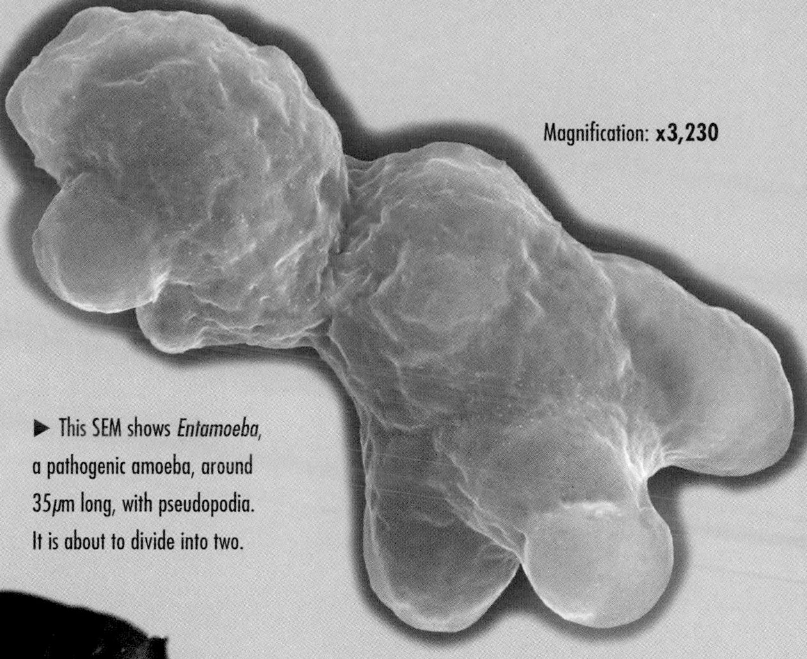

Magnification: **x3,230**

► This SEM shows *Entamoeba*, a pathogenic amoeba, around 35µm long, with pseudopodia. It is about to divide into two.

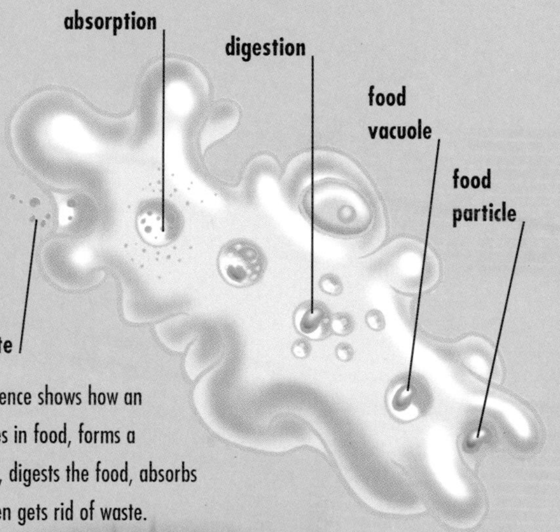

absorption

digestion

food vacuole

food particle

waste

► This sequence shows how an amoeba takes in food, forms a food vacuole, digests the food, absorbs nutrients, then gets rid of waste.

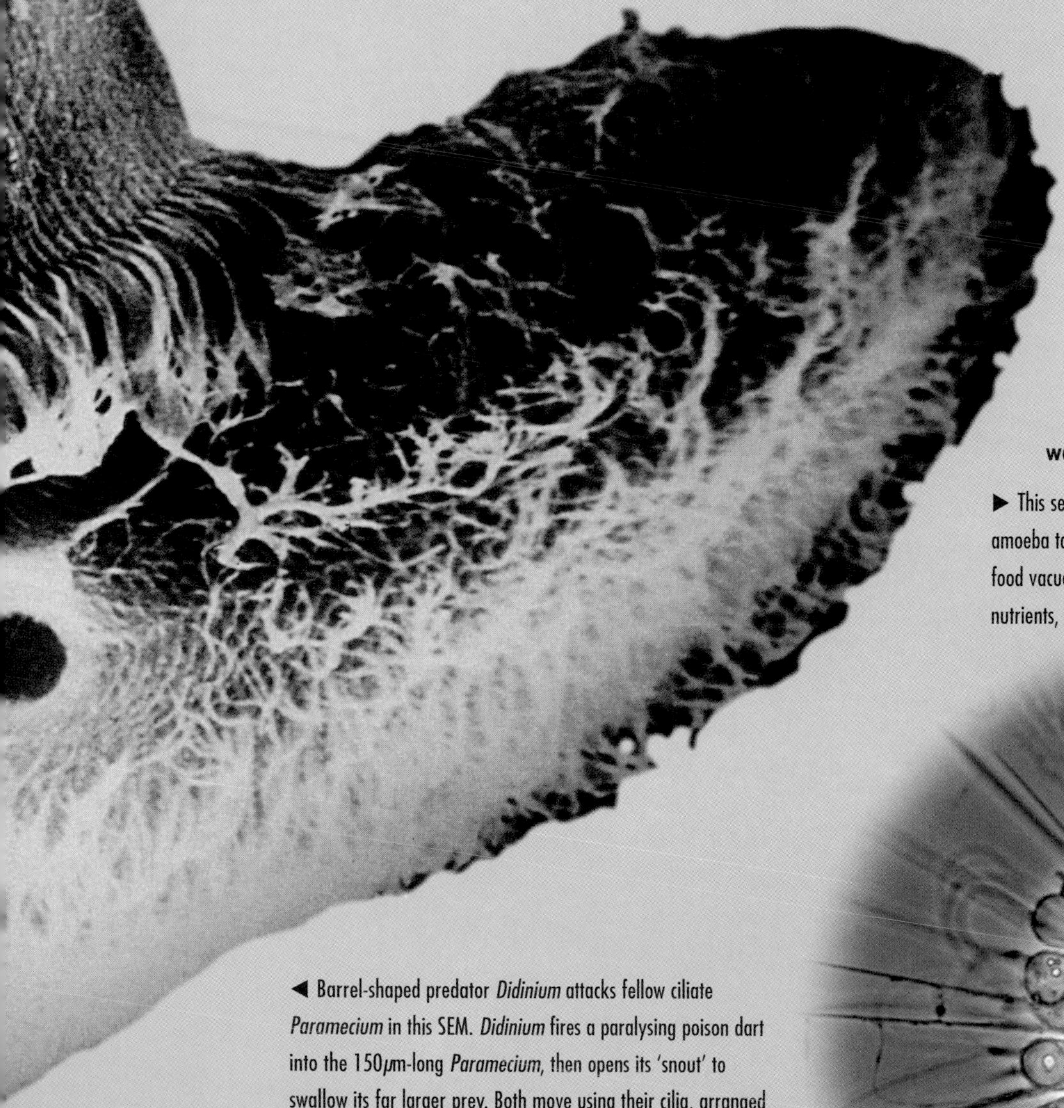

Magnification: **x2,130**

◄ Barrel-shaped predator *Didinium* attacks fellow ciliate *Paramecium* in this SEM. *Didinium* fires a paralysing poison dart into the 150µm-long *Paramecium*, then opens its 'snout' to swallow its far larger prey. Both move using their cilia, arranged in two 'belts' in *Didinium* and a complete covering in *Paramecium*.

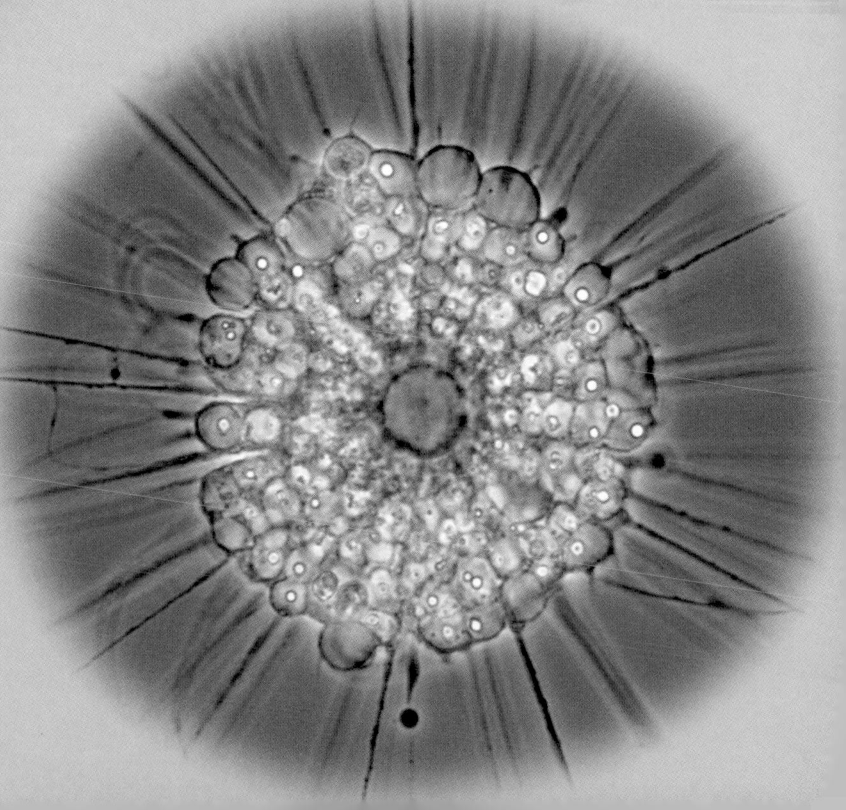

► Heliozoans, or 'sun animals', are freshwater and marine amoeboids that resemble a shining sun. Freshwater *Actinophrys*, seen in this LM, has a 'body' 50µm across, and uses its needle-like pseudopodia, called axopodia, to move and to capture food. Magnification: **x120**

Fungi

Neither plant nor animal, fungi form a group of living things that includes mushrooms, toadstools and puffballs, as well as mildews on plants, mould on bread, and yeasts. But, if nearly all of these fungi can be seen without a microscope, why should they be included in this book? There are three reasons. Firstly because although large fungi look smooth, they are actually made up of a mass of microscopic threads. Secondly because of they way they feed, and finally because of the tiny spores they release in order to reproduce.

Feeding threads

Fungi do not make food using sunlight, as plants and algae do, nor do they roam in search of food and then eat it, as many animals do. Instead, fungi feed through microscopic threads called hyphae that grow through a food source. The network of fungal hyphae – called a mycelium – releases enzymes, chemicals that digest or break down the chosen food into a soup of simple nutrients which are absorbed into the hyphae. The mycelium of a bread mould (below) spreads through bread, while that of a mushroom can extend through the soil of an entire field. Most fungi, such as mushrooms and moulds, are saprobes – they feed on dead animal and plant material. But some are parasites, feeding on living organisms and causing diseases such as athlete's foot in humans, and mildews and rusts in plants.

▶ Like most fungi, this puffball, *Lycoperdon pyriforme* (also known as the wolf-fart puffball), reproduces by forming spores that are spread through the air. As can be seen here, puffballs force out clouds of millions of microscopic spores through an opening in the top of their fruiting body.

◀ This slice of bread is almost unrecognizable because it has a covering of woolly bread mould. Tangled hyphae can be seen here growing upwards from the bread, at the top of which are black, spherical fruiting bodies. These burst open to release tiny spores.
Magnification: **x12**

Magnification:
x3,800

'parent' cell

'daughter' cell
budding off

▲ These grapes are covered in a greyish waxy
layer made by millions of yeast cells, which feed on
sugary juices that ooze out through the grapes' skins.

◀ This SEM shows yeast cells, the
largest being about 10μm across.

Single cells

Not all fungi are made of hyphae. Yeasts are microscopic
fungi that exist as individual single cells. They reproduce
by a process called budding. A 'parent' yeast cell produces
a new cell, or bud (above left) that remains attached to the
parent and then separates to lead its own life. Yeast cells
absorb nutrients directly from their surroundings. Those
living on fruit, for example, obtain energy from the sugar-
rich juices and release carbon dioxide. This process is used
in bread-making (see page 38). Some yeasts are parasites,
such as the one that causes the disease thrush in humans.

Billions of spores

The hyphae of most fungi grow invisibly through food
sources including bread, soil, wallpaper paste, floorboards,
bird droppings, fallen leaves, fruit or living animal and plant
tissues. But, in order to reproduce, fungi form visible
fruiting bodies that release microscopic spores into the air.
In microscopic moulds, these fruiting bodies are spheres
that cap woolly growths of hyphae and burst to release
their contents. In larger forms, a tightly packed mycelium
of hyphae forms a puffball (left) from which billions of
spores can be released in a short time. In every case, the
minute spores, each containing one or two fungal cells,
float in the air. Those that land on a suitable food source
will germinate there and grow into a new fungus.

Mini-animals

Mention the word 'animal' to someone, and they will probably think of something easily visible such as a lion or a bee. But there are plenty of microscopic animals – let's call them mini-animals – that live unnoticed by us. They include *Hydra* (a relative of sea anemones), minute crustaceans (relatives of crabs and lobsters), tiny mites and pseudoscorpions (the cousins of spiders), and mini-insects, as well as many other animal types. Like their larger relatives, mini-animals are made up of lots of cells and live by taking in food, either plants or other animals, or both. Mini-animals are found everywhere, but here we look at three habitats – soil, water and our homes.

Magnification: **x17.5**

▲ Less than 3mm long, pseudoscorpions live in leaf-litter. Like scorpions, their larger, distant relatives, they have claws, but they lack the scorpion's curved tail and sting.

In the soil

Soil and leaf-litter (rotting leaf and plant material on the soil) are swarming with mini-animals. Along with soil fungi and bacteria, primitive insects such as springtails and proturans feed on dead animals and plants. A handful of soil contains millions of microscopic worms called roundworms, which have smooth, cylindrical bodies. They feed on rotting material, as well as fungi and plant roots. There are hunters here as well. Pseudoscorpions ('false scorpions') track down prey by touch, then use their pincers to grab and inject poison into their prey before sucking out the juices from the paralysed victim.

bud

Magnification: **x140**

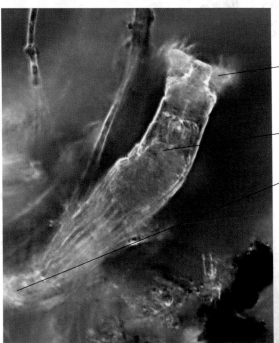

circle of cilia

stomach

toe

◄ Around 0.5mm long, rotifers, or wheel animals, live in freshwater ponds. This one is attached to a plant by its 'toe'. The rotifer's head has two circles of hair-like cilia that beat like revolving wheels, making currents that draw food particles into its mouth and stomach. Magnification: **x150**

In water

A whole new world of animal life is revealed by putting a drop of pond water under the microscope. Near the surface are zooplankton (see also pages 54–55), tiny animals that feed on tinier animals or plants and, in turn, provide food for larger animals. Some are larvae that will grow into bigger adults. Others, including *Cyclops* – which locates its food (algae and dead animals) by touch – spend their lives here. Some other pond animals, such as rotifers and *Hydra*, live fixed to plants or stones. *Hydra* grabs passing prey using its armed tentacles. It reproduces by growing a bud which eventually drops off to form a new individual.

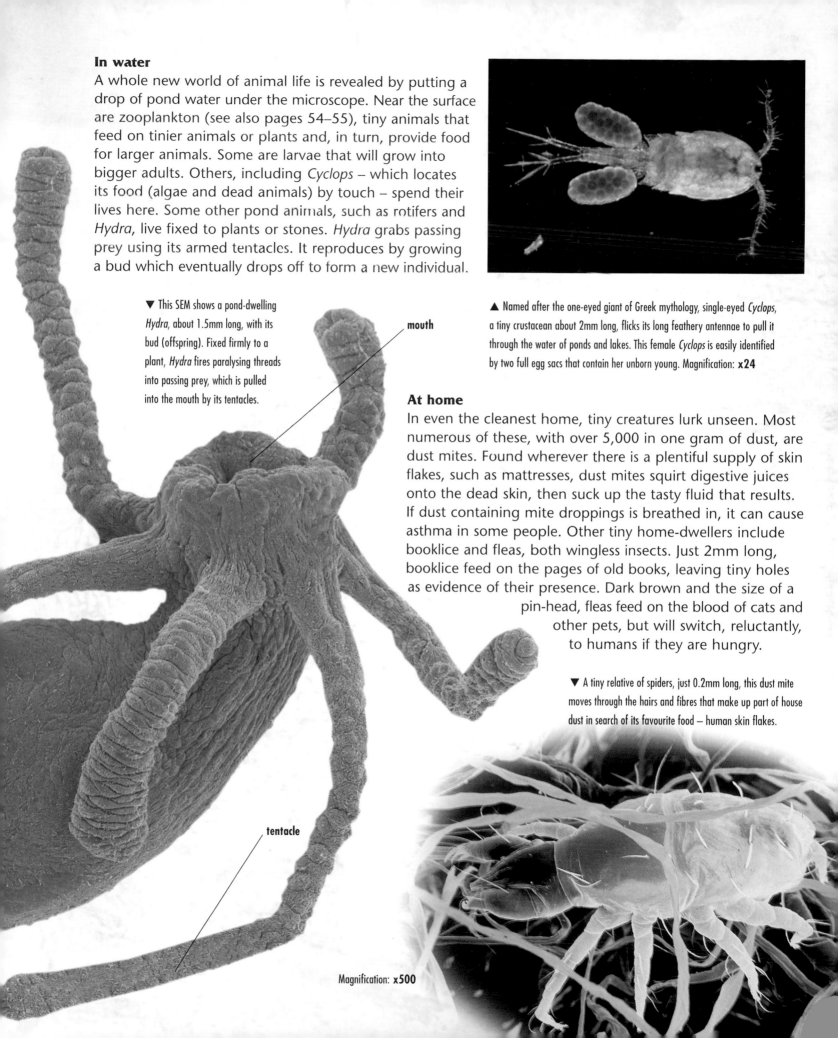

▼ This SEM shows a pond-dwelling *Hydra*, about 1.5mm long, with its bud (offspring). Fixed firmly to a plant, *Hydra* fires paralysing threads into passing prey, which is pulled into the mouth by its tentacles.

mouth

tentacle

Magnification: **x500**

▲ Named after the one-eyed giant of Greek mythology, single-eyed *Cyclops*, a tiny crustacean about 2mm long, flicks its long feathery antennae to pull it through the water of ponds and lakes. This female *Cyclops* is easily identified by two full egg sacs that contain her unborn young. Magnification: **x24**

At home

In even the cleanest home, tiny creatures lurk unseen. Most numerous of these, with over 5,000 in one gram of dust, are dust mites. Found wherever there is a plentiful supply of skin flakes, such as mattresses, dust mites squirt digestive juices onto the dead skin, then suck up the tasty fluid that results. If dust containing mite droppings is breathed in, it can cause asthma in some people. Other tiny home-dwellers include booklice and fleas, both wingless insects. Just 2mm long, booklice feed on the pages of old books, leaving tiny holes as evidence of their presence. Dark brown and the size of a pin-head, fleas feed on the blood of cats and other pets, but will switch, reluctantly, to humans if they are hungry.

▼ A tiny relative of spiders, just 0.2mm long, this dust mite moves through the hairs and fibres that make up part of house dust in search of its favourite food — human skin flakes.

SUMMARY OF CHAPTER 2: MICROSCOPIC ORGANISMS

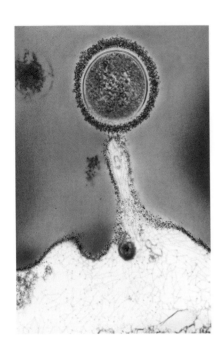

TEM of a *Streptococcus* bacterium attached to a tonsil cell (blue) in the throat
Magnification: **x33,000**

Micro-variety

The microscopic world is packed with variety. The microscopic organisms that inhabit it are mostly unicellular (consisting of a single cell) but there are also multicellular (many-celled) species. To make sense of this mass of microlife we order it into categories based on the way these organisms look and live.

Packages, prokaryotes and protists

Viruses, the simplest of microbes, are chemical packages surrounded by a protective coat. They barely qualify as life forms because they neither feed nor move, and can reproduce only by infecting a living cell. Each virus package is a set of instructions that creates more viruses – these instructions are set into motion when the virus infects a living cell. Bacteria, the most numerous and widespread organisms on earth, consist of a single, prokaryotic cell – a specific bacterial cell that has no nucleus, unlike cells of other organisms. Protists – the plant-like algae and animal-like protozoa – are bigger than bacteria and inhabit water and damp places.

Small and large

Two other groups of living things – fungi and animals – include some species that are microscopic (yeasts and rotifers) and others that are big (puffballs and elephants). Microscopic fungi, along with viruses, bacteria and protists, are grouped together as micro-organisms and studied by microbiologists. Fungi feed through tiny threads called hyphae that grow through a food source. In this book, microscopic animals are called mini-animals. Mini-animals feed by taking in food as their larger relatives do.

Go further...

Visit the 'smallest' page on the web to examine the bacteria, protists and mini-animals in a drop of water:
www.microscopy-uk.org.uk/mag/wimsmall/smal1.html

The National Geographic 'Bacteria Rule' website gives information about bugs and germs at:
http://nationalgeographic.com/world/0010/bacteria

For a really clear account of microbes go to:
www.microbe.org/microbes/what_is.asp and www.microbe.org

Megabites Microlife by David Burnie (Dorling Kindersley, 2002)

Bacteriologist
Microbiologist who specializes in the study of bacteria.

Mycologist
Explores the biology and uses of moulds, yeasts and other fungi.

Parasitologist
Studies the structure, biochemistry and life cycles of parasites.

Protozoologist
Studies animal-like protists (protozoa).

Virologist
Microbiologist who studies viruses, the diseases they cause and how they infect cells.

The Traits of Life exhibition at the Exploratorium covers many microscopic life forms:
The Palace of Fine Arts,
3601 Lyon Street, San Francisco,
CA 94123, USA
Telephone: +1 415 561 0308
www.exploratorium.edu

See the Hidden Kingdoms – The World of Microbes exhibition at:
New York Hall of Science,
47–01 111th Street, Queens,
NY 11368, USA
Telephone: +1 718 699 0005
www.nyhallsci.org

CHAPTER 3

Inside the microworld

A look inside the microworld reveals much about how microbes live and work. In fact, the more we discover about these tiny organisms, the more we realize how much they affect not only our lives but those of all living things on earth. As Louis Pasteur wrote in 1869, 'The role of the infinitely small is infinitely large'. While it is true that throughout

history micro-organisms have had a negative impact on humans and other organisms by causing disease, today we recognize how much many microbes help us and our fellow organisms. Put simply, without the microworld, life could not exist.

A colony of the mould *Penicillium notatum* grows on nutrient medium. The discovery in 1928 by Alexander Fleming that a substance released by this fungus killed bacteria led eventually to production of penicillin, the first antibiotic.
Magnification: **x4**

Virus alert

Viruses are parasitic packages of chemicals that have to take over the cells of living organisms in order to reproduce themselves. Many cause diseases ranging from mild to very serious. We depend on our built-in immune, or defence, system to destroy invading viruses before they destroy us. Today, we can be protected from known viral diseases such as measles or rubella by vaccination, which 'boosts' our immune system. But viruses change and we need to be always alert for newer, deadlier versions.

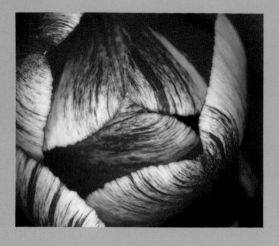

▲ A virus has given yellow streaks to this normally all-red tulip flower. Viral infection passes from one generation to the next, and is prized by gardeners because of the colourful patterns it makes.

Causing disease

Virus infections can have harmless results, such as altering a flower's colour. But generally viruses cause disease, as they multiply and burst out from infected cells. Mild infections, such as colds, are easily overcome. Others, such as mumps and measles, are normally defeated by the immune system. But viruses can change their 'identity', producing new, more dangerous, strains that the immune system cannot identify. In 1918–19, a new flu strain caused a world-wide epidemic that killed over 20 million people – many more deaths than occurred during World War I (1914–18).

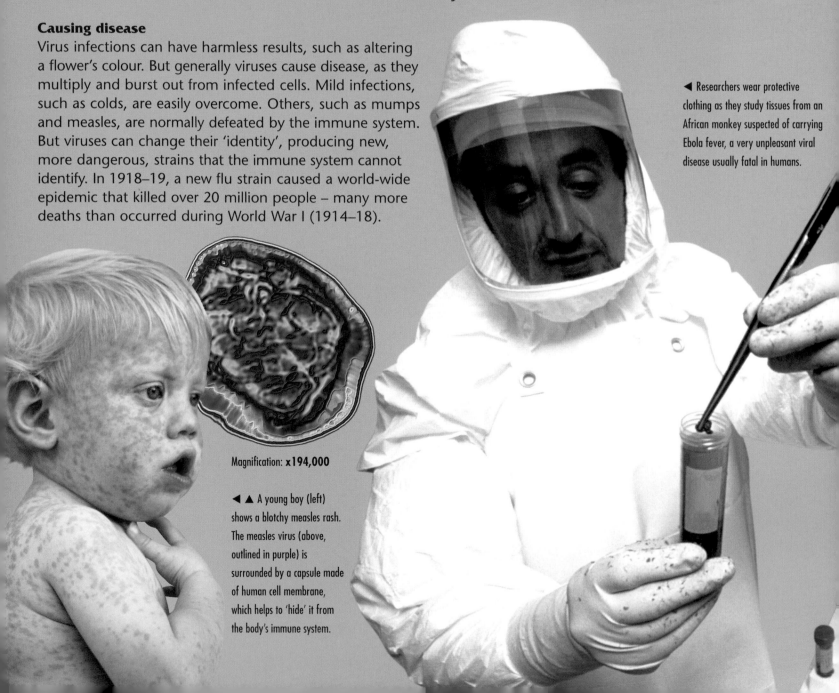

◄ Researchers wear protective clothing as they study tissues from an African monkey suspected of carrying Ebola fever, a very unpleasant viral disease usually fatal in humans.

Magnification: x194,000

◄ ▲ A young boy (left) shows a blotchy measles rash. The measles virus (above, outlined in purple) is surrounded by a capsule made of human cell membrane, which helps to 'hide' it from the body's immune system.

Tropical diseases

Yellow fever is a tropical disease, sometimes fatal, that takes its name from the yellowing of the skin which results from the virus damaging a person's liver. In the 19th century, yellow fever was a serious problem in Central America. Its cause remained unknown until 1900 when US Army doctor Walter Reed (1851–1902) and his team, working in Cuba, showed that yellow fever is caused by a virus and spread by mosquitoes. Today, people can be protected against yellow fever by vaccination, but the same is not true for some of the viral haemmorrhagic (bleeding) fevers. In central Africa, for example, outbreaks of Ebola fever occur when the virus spreads from monkeys to humans, or humans to humans. The disease causes massive internal bleeding and usually results in death.

▶ A female *Aedes aegypti* mosquito pushes her needle-like mouthparts through skin to feed on blood. Each time they feed, these mosquitoes may pass on one of two different tropical viral diseases – flu-like dengue or more deadly yellow fever – picked up from another person's blood.

Magnification: **x8**

Destroying defences

Some viruses target the immune system. They include HIV (Human Immunodeficiency Virus), identified in 1983, which causes AIDS (Acquired Immune Deficiency Syndrome). Key to our immune system are lymphocytes – cells that identify and destroy germs. HIV invades and multiplies inside the lymphocytes. This weakens a person's immune system and, eventually, they develop AIDS – a condition in which the body is unable to fight off even common diseases. The body is overwhelmed by infection and the person dies. There is no cure for AIDS at present, but certain drugs can slow the progress of HIV infection.

▶ Seen in detail, 100nm-across, HIV has 'spikes' (yellow) that attach to lymphocytes.

▼ This SEM shows a human lymphocyte (green) infected with HIV, with new viruses (red) emerging from its surface.

Magnification: **x520,000**

Magnification: **x7,300**

Bacteria – enemies or friends?

Bacteria affect our lives in very many ways. Some are harmful and make us ill. But others release life-giving oxygen into the air, or recycle dead organisms to maintain a balance of nutrients in the air and soil. Other bacteria are used to make foods, such as cheese, as well as drugs and other useful chemicals. Without bacteria, plants, humans and other animals simply could not exist.

Harmful bacteria

Some types of bacteria live on or in living things. Many are harmless and some even help us, but others, known as pathogens or germs, can cause disease in animals and plants if they get into their tissues. In humans, pathogenic bacteria cause serious diseases, including typhoid, tuberculosis (TB), plague and meningitis, as well as milder conditions such as acne and tooth decay. Pathogenic bacteria usually harm an organism by releasing poisonous chemicals called toxins, which may disrupt cell activities or even destroy cells. Botulinum toxin, released by *Clostridium botulinum*, causes serious food poisoning called botulism in humans. It is the deadliest natural poison known – one drop could kill 100,000 people.

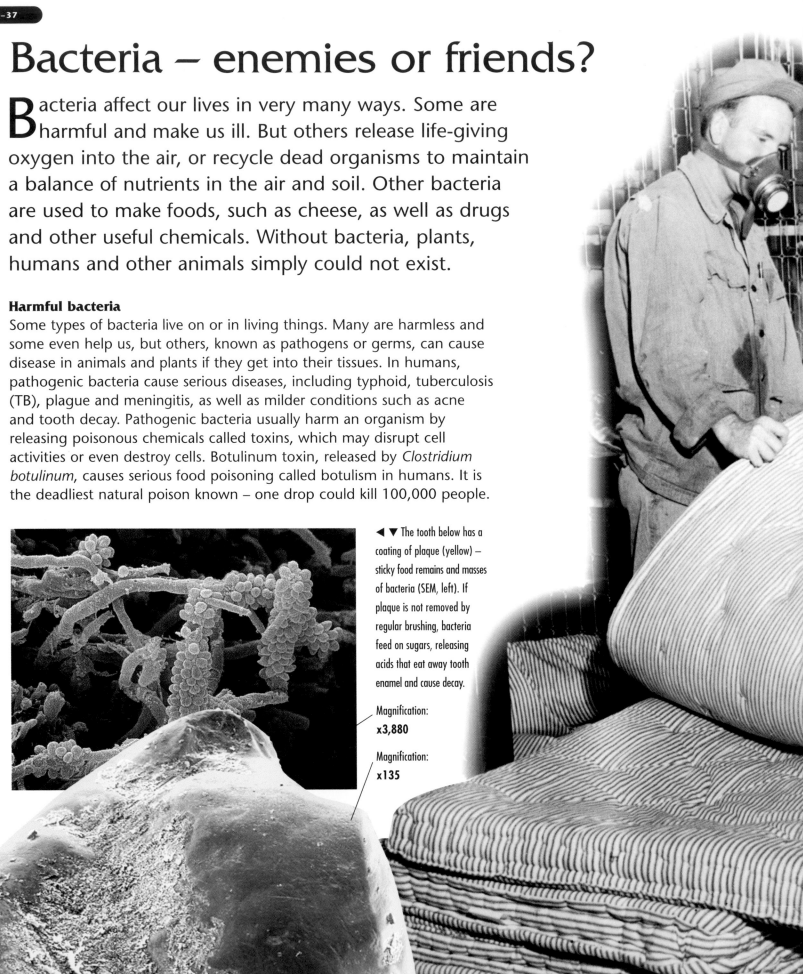

◄ ▼ The tooth below has a coating of plaque (yellow) – sticky food remains and masses of bacteria (SEM, left). If plaque is not removed by regular brushing, bacteria feed on sugars, releasing acids that eat away tooth enamel and cause decay.

Magnification:
x3,880

Magnification:
x135

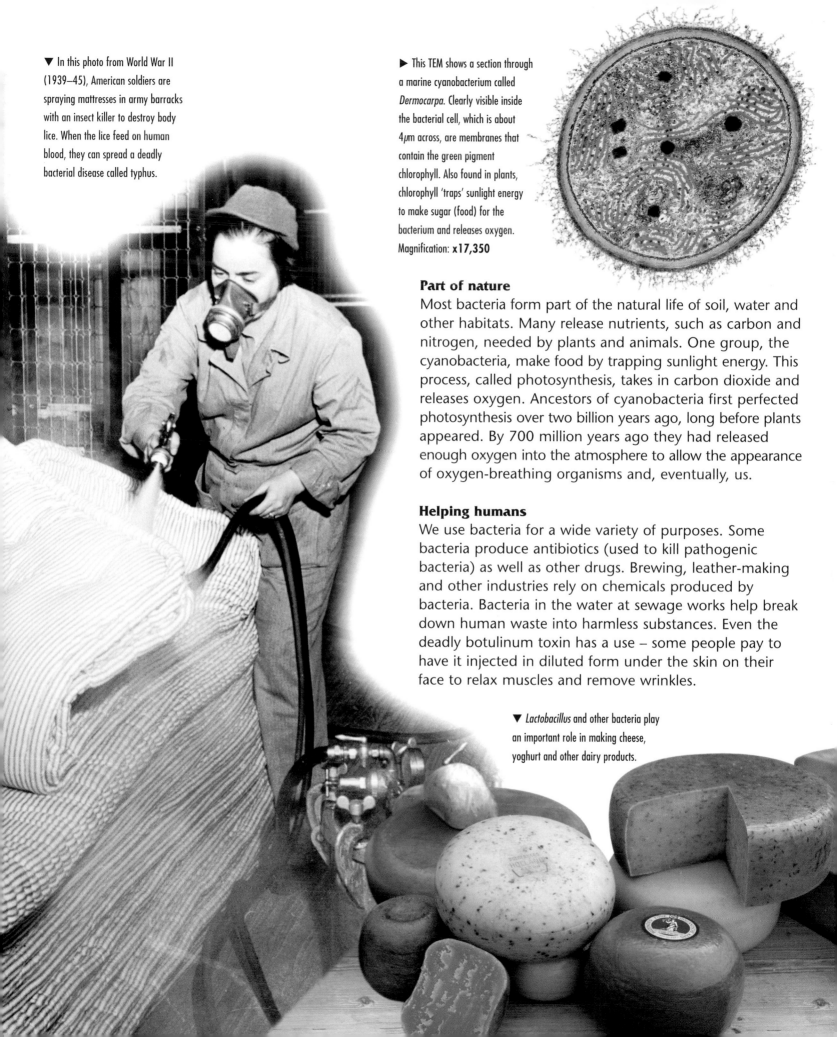

▼ In this photo from World War II (1939–45), American soldiers are spraying mattresses in army barracks with an insect killer to destroy body lice. When the lice feed on human blood, they can spread a deadly bacterial disease called typhus.

▶ This TEM shows a section through a marine cyanobacterium called *Dermocarpa*. Clearly visible inside the bacterial cell, which is about 4μm across, are membranes that contain the green pigment chlorophyll. Also found in plants, chlorophyll 'traps' sunlight energy to make sugar (food) for the bacterium and releases oxygen.
Magnification: **x17,350**

Part of nature

Most bacteria form part of the natural life of soil, water and other habitats. Many release nutrients, such as carbon and nitrogen, needed by plants and animals. One group, the cyanobacteria, make food by trapping sunlight energy. This process, called photosynthesis, takes in carbon dioxide and releases oxygen. Ancestors of cyanobacteria first perfected photosynthesis over two billion years ago, long before plants appeared. By 700 million years ago they had released enough oxygen into the atmosphere to allow the appearance of oxygen-breathing organisms and, eventually, us.

Helping humans

We use bacteria for a wide variety of purposes. Some bacteria produce antibiotics (used to kill pathogenic bacteria) as well as other drugs. Brewing, leather-making and other industries rely on chemicals produced by bacteria. Bacteria in the water at sewage works help break down human waste into harmless substances. Even the deadly botulinum toxin has a use – some people pay to have it injected in diluted form under the skin on their face to relax muscles and remove wrinkles.

▼ *Lactobacillus* and other bacteria play an important role in making cheese, yoghurt and other dairy products.

▲ Bread dough is left to rise in a warm place before being baked in the oven. Dough contains yeast, a single-celled fungus. Yeast breaks down sugar to obtain energy, releasing carbon-dioxide gas which makes the dough rise and gives bread lightness.

Fungi at work

Carried by the air, microscopic fungal spores grow into new fungi when they land on their preferred source of food. Here they get to work, using threads called hyphae that penetrate and digest dead or living organisms, then soak up the nutrients which are released. By working this way, fungi affect us humans in many ways, some helpful and some harmful. We use fungi as food and to provide drugs. Fungi play a part in natural cycles of life to make dead things rot and release essential nutrients for new generations, but this rotting ability also damages our everyday materials. Fungi can make us ill, and cause disease in other animals and plants.

Helpful fungi

Microscopic yeasts feed on sugars to release both carbon-dioxide gas – used to make bread rise – and ethanol (alcohol) – used to make drinks such as beer and wine. Mushrooms and their relatives are eaten in all kinds of foods. Moulds, such as *Penicillium*, give Roquefort and other blue cheeses their blue streaks, and Camembert and Brie their distinctive tastes. Fungi are also used to make soy sauce and to turn soya beans into the vegetable protein tofu. We use fungi to make bacteria-killing antibiotic drugs such as penicillin, and other drugs including cyclosporin, used to stop a body rejecting transplanted organs, such as kidneys.

▼ ▶ The fungal disease athlete's foot (below) produces itchy, sore and cracked skin on the toes. The SEM (right) shows branching hyphae (orange) of *Trichophyton mentagrophytes*, one of the fungi that causes athlete's foot, spreading among skin flakes. The fungus feeds on keratin, a tough protein found in skin flakes and in the skin's outer layer, the epidermis. Athlete's foot can be treated using anti-fungal creams.

Magnification: x4,350

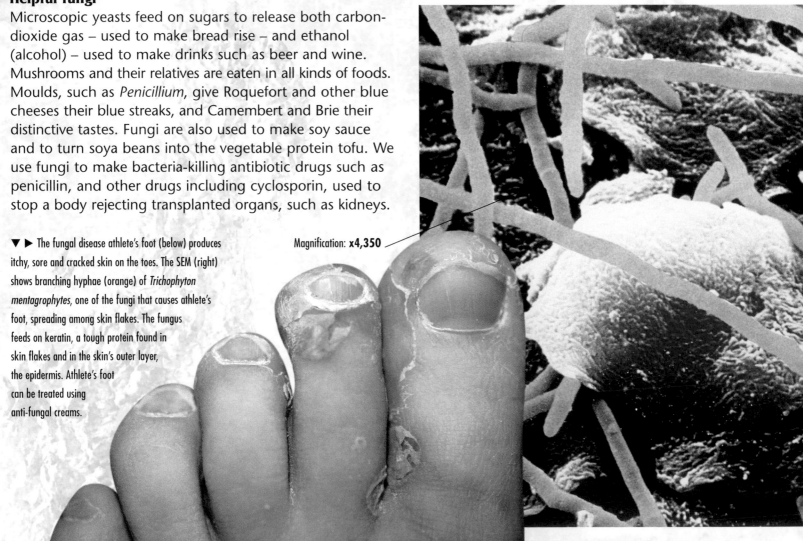

▲ This timber is badly affected by *Serpula lacrymans*, a fungus that causes dry rot. Its thick bundles of hyphae spread over long distances feeding on damp timber until the wood eventually crumbles. The only remedy is to cut out rotting timber and spray the area to prevent further attack.

Decomposers

In forests, fields and other habitats, fungi play a vital role by helping to break down, or decompose, dead plant and animal remains. These decomposers release vital nutrients that plants and animals need to grow and thrive. But decomposing fungi make no distinction between, say, a rotting tree in a forest and the floorboards in our houses. The dry rot fungus, for example, grows rapidly in damp conditions and quickly destroys floors unless treated. Other types of fungi rot fresh fruit, meat, bread, vegetables and other foods, making them mouldy and inedible. These food feeders include a fungus that attacks stored cereals and peanuts, and releases a poison called aflatoxin that kills thousands of people every year. Fungi can also attack and ruin most of the materials we use in everyday life, including paper, clothes, leather, paint, petrol and film.

Causing disease

Pathogenic fungi are those that cause disease by feeding on living, not dead, plants and animals. Over 5,000 types of fungi, including the rusts, smuts and mildews, attack economically important food crops, such as wheat and corn, and make them inedible or poisonous. Fungi also infect, damage and kill trees and garden plants, such as roses. Other pathogenic fungi cause diseases in humans and other animals. Ringworm is caused by a ring-shaped, itchy fungal growth on the skin of the body or head. Thrush, or candidiasis, is caused by a white growth of a yeast in body openings such as the mouth.

▶ The brown dusty marks seen in this close-up view of an ear of wheat are caused by *Puccinia graminis*, one of the 'rust' fungi. Rusts cause great damage to crops such as wheat and can result in heavy losses for farmers.

Infection and defence

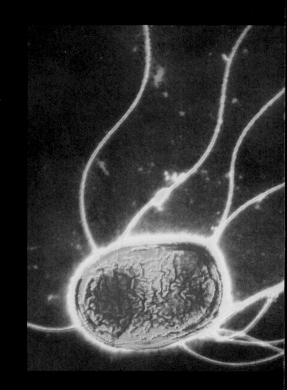

People fight a constant battle to avoid invasion by a hostile army of pathogens, or germs. These are the micro-organisms that cause infectious diseases. Once a pathogen gets inside the body, it causes an infection by growing rapidly and multiplying, which disrupts how the body works. An infected person shows symptoms and signs that are typical of the pathogen and the disease it causes. To prevent invasion by pathogens, the body has a series of barriers that form its outer defences. Pathogens that manage to get through these barriers are usually then destroyed by the body's inner defences.

Routes of infection

Pathogens arrive on, or in, the body by different routes, often from another person who is infected. Many diseases, such as chickenpox and colds, are spread when a person breathes in pathogens contained in droplets released from another infected person by a sneeze or cough. Some, such as cold sores, are spread by direct touch between people. A few, including malaria, are spread by biting insects as they move from person to person feeding on blood. Lastly, diseases, such as food poisoning, are caused by eating food or drinking water contaminated by pathogens from human and farm animal faeces.

Outer defences

To cause infection, a pathogen first has to breach the body's outer defences. Skin is a watertight, germ-proof barrier that protects the body's insides. Sweat, tears and saliva all contain antiseptic (germ-killing) chemicals. The nose and mouth are lined with tightly packed cells, like paving stones, that stop pathogens penetrating to the tissues below. The windpipe is coated with sticky mucus that traps airborne pathogens, which are then carried up to the throat and swallowed. In the stomach, these pathogens are destroyed by powerfully acidic stomach juices.

▼ The tiny droplets forced out by this sneeze may contain coronaviruses (right, orange), each just 100nm across, that cause the common cold. If breathed in by another person, the viruses invade cells inside the nose and throat, causing a stuffy, runny nose and sore throat. Magnification: **x235,300**

Magnification: **x1,175**

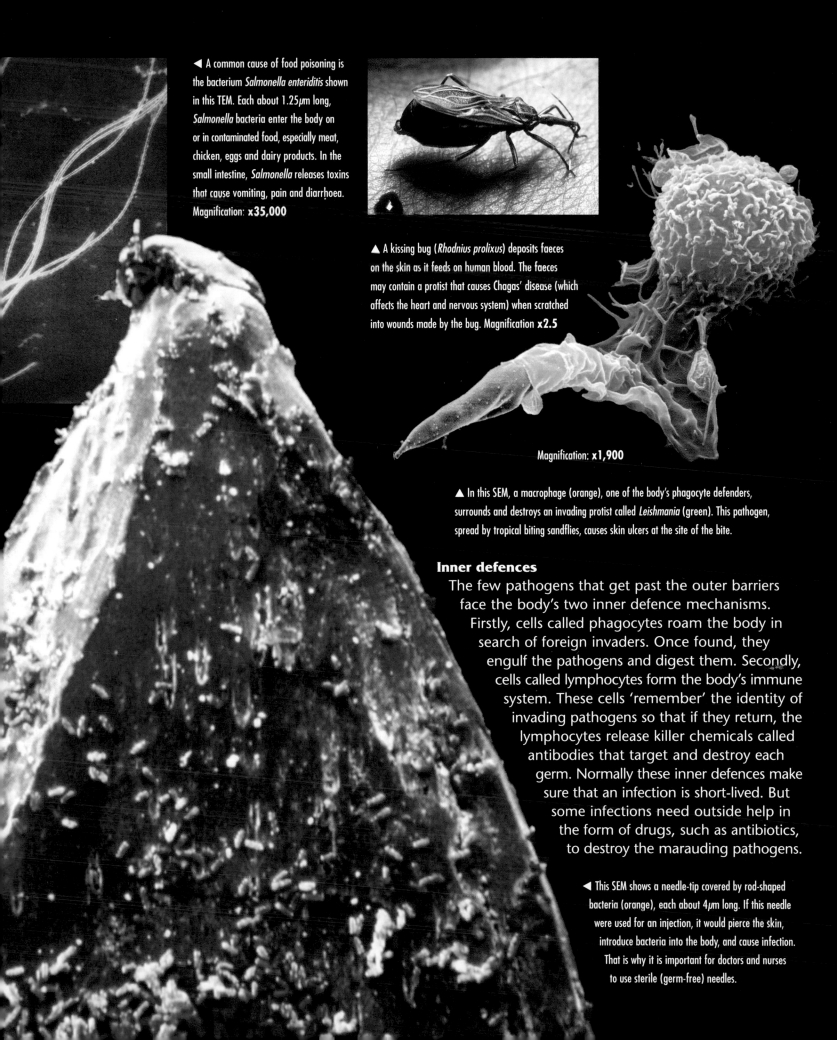

◄ A common cause of food poisoning is the bacterium *Salmonella enteriditis* shown in this TEM. Each about 1.25μm long, *Salmonella* bacteria enter the body on or in contaminated food, especially meat, chicken, eggs and dairy products. In the small intestine, *Salmonella* releases toxins that cause vomiting, pain and diarrhoea. Magnification: **x35,000**

▲ A kissing bug (*Rhodnius prolixus*) deposits faeces on the skin as it feeds on human blood. The faeces may contain a protist that causes Chagas' disease (which affects the heart and nervous system) when scratched into wounds made by the bug. Magnification **x2.5**

Magnification: **x1,900**

▲ In this SEM, a macrophage (orange), one of the body's phagocyte defenders, surrounds and destroys an invading protist called *Leishmania* (green). This pathogen, spread by tropical biting sandflies, causes skin ulcers at the site of the bite.

Inner defences

The few pathogens that get past the outer barriers face the body's two inner defence mechanisms. Firstly, cells called phagocytes roam the body in search of foreign invaders. Once found, they engulf the pathogens and digest them. Secondly, cells called lymphocytes form the body's immune system. These cells 'remember' the identity of invading pathogens so that if they return, the lymphocytes release killer chemicals called antibodies that target and destroy each germ. Normally these inner defences make sure that an infection is short-lived. But some infections need outside help in the form of drugs, such as antibiotics, to destroy the marauding pathogens.

◄ This SEM shows a needle-tip covered by rod-shaped bacteria (orange), each about 4μm long. If this needle were used for an injection, it would pierce the skin, introduce bacteria into the body, and cause infection. That is why it is important for doctors and nurses to use sterile (germ-free) needles.

Great epidemics

An epidemic happens when an infectious disease spreads rapidly to affect large numbers of people. For example, influenza (flu) epidemics happen every few years and many people, especially in cities, become ill. Most people recover, but this was not the case in the great epidemics of the past. Smallpox, plague, cholera, measles and tuberculosis (TB) were just some of the diseases that killed millions of people. But until the 19th and 20th centuries, no one understood the causes of these diseases, let alone how to treat them.

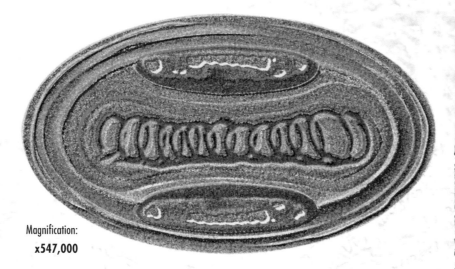

▶ Just 0.2µm across, a variola virus, the cause of smallpox, is shown in this computer-generated image. Like many other viruses, variola has an outer protein coat and a central core of DNA. Although smallpox has been destroyed, the variola virus is still used for scientific research.

Magnification:
x547,000

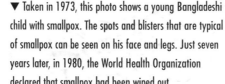

▼ Taken in 1973, this photo shows a young Bangladeshi child with smallpox. The spots and blisters that are typical of smallpox can be seen on his face and legs. Just seven years later, in 1980, the World Health Organization declared that smallpox had been wiped out.

The scourge of smallpox

Known since the earliest times, smallpox was a major killer. Caused by the variola virus, smallpox spread easily from person to person. An infected person had a fever, then a rash that developed into pus-filled blisters that often scarred those who survived. Particularly at risk were those people who had no natural immunity. When, for example, the Spanish conquistadors arrived in Central America in 1519, they brought smallpox with them. Epidemics spread through the defenceless native Americans, reducing their population from 30 to three million in just 50 years. In the 18th century, vaccination was first used to prevent smallpox, and in the late 1970s the disease was finally eliminated.

This 17th-century doctor wears a beaked mask. The beak was filled with strong-smelling herbs that covered up the stench of dead and decaying bodies. Also, not knowing how plague spread from person to person, some doctors believed that the strong herbal aromas could protect them from infection.

▲ This woodcut of the Great Plague of 1665 shows the dead being buried outside the walls of the City of London.

Death by plague

Plague is caused by a bacterium called *Yersinia pestis*. It is mainly a disease of rats, spread from rat to rat by the fleas that feed on their blood. But when rats die of the disease, the infected fleas feed on people and spread the disease to them. These facts were unknown when an outbreak of plague, called the Black Death, spread from Asia and killed one-third of Europe's population in the late 1340s. Victims developed large dark swellings, or buboes, and most died a painful death soon afterwards. Another plague epidemic in London in 1665 killed up to 100,000 people. Today, plague is rare and can usually be treated with bacteria-killing drugs.

◀ This painting shows Dr Edward Jenner carrying out his first vaccination against smallpox in 1796.

Giving protection

Smallpox was a deadly disease with no cure. But Edward Jenner (1749–1823), an English doctor, noticed that milkmaids who caught the related but less harmful disease cowpox from their cows never caught smallpox. This gave him an idea. In 1796, he infected eight-year-old James Phipps with cowpox by scraping pus from a cowpox blister into his arm. Six weeks later, Jenner infected the boy with smallpox, but James did not develop this disease. His immune system had been triggered by cowpox to form a defensive shield against smallpox. In this way, James Phipps experienced the first vaccination.

▼ Scottish bacteriologist Alexander Fleming in his London laboratory in 1943. He holds a Petri dish containing *Penicillium* mould.

Microbe fighters

Although Antony van Leeuwenhoek had seen and described bacteria as far back as 1683, by the mid 19th century doctors and scientists had not made the link between microbes and disease. Most believed that diseases were caused and spread by poisonous air that arose from stagnant ponds and human waste. Then a series of discoveries revealed not only that many diseases were caused by bacteria and viruses, but also showed how to fight and destroy these microbes. First, let us return to the 18th century.

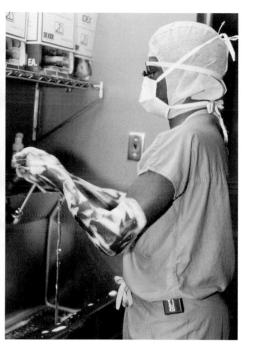

Germ Theory

Vaccination protected James, but nobody knew why. Neither, in 1846, did Austrian doctor Ignaz Semmelweiss (1818–65) understand why insisting that his fellow doctors washed their blood- and pus-covered hands before treating patients greatly reduced death rates from infection. Other doctors even made fun of Semmelweiss for suggesting that infection could be carried on their hands! Eventually, answers were provided by the French microbiologist Louis Pasteur (1822–95) and the German doctor Robert Koch (1843–1910) from the 1860s onwards. Their Germ Theory proved conclusively that specific bacteria and, later, certain viruses cause specific diseases. Semmelweiss was finally proved right – washing dirty hands does remove harmful bacteria.

▲ A surgeon scrubs his arms and hands before an operation to remove germs that might infect his patient. Cleanliness in hospitals is seen as vital to prevent infection, just as Dr Ignaz Semmelweiss had suggested in the 1840s, but was ignored.

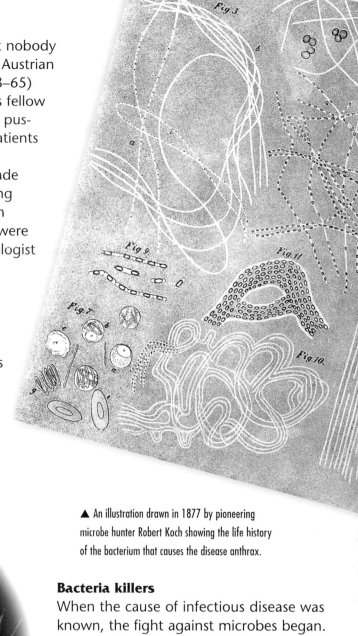

▲ An illustration drawn in 1877 by pioneering microbe hunter Robert Koch showing the life history of the bacterium that causes the disease anthrax.

Bacteria killers

When the cause of infectious disease was known, the fight against microbes began. In 1865, English surgeon Joseph Lister (1827–1912) used carbolic acid spray to kill micro-organisms during operations. At this time in America and Europe, sewers were built to remove waste and prevent the contamination of drinking water by harmful bacteria. Then the search for microbe-killing drugs began. Perhaps the most significant find happened in 1928 when bacteriologist Alexander Fleming (1881–1955) found that a chemical (penicillin) released by a mould called *Penicillium* killed disease-causing bacteria. Full-scale production of penicillin began in the 1940s. Since then, penicillin and other antibiotics (bacteria-killing drugs) have saved the lives of millions of people.

Microbes as partners

Micro-organisms sometimes form partnerships with other living things in a close relationship called symbiosis ('living together'). Symbiotic relationships take different forms, including mutualism and parasitism. Mutualism is a relationship in which both partners benefit, and neither can survive without the other. Microbes in a mutual relationship help their larger partner, or host, in return for a safe place to live. Parasitism (see pages 48–49), on the other hand, benefits just one partner (the microbe) at the expense of another and often causes disease.

Wood eaters

Many animals feed on plants, and the chief part of their diet is the substance cellulose, the main component of a plant's supporting framework. However, most plant-eaters cannot digest energy-rich cellulose. They can only gain benefit from this valuable food source through a partnership with cellulose-digesting micro-organisms. Termites, for example, are insects that feed on wood and live in large colonies. The termites that forage for food are called workers. Living inside each worker's gut are many thousands of protists, particularly *Trichonympha*. They digest the tiny cellulose-rich wood chips which the worker swallows and release the nutrients that allow the termite, and colony, to live.

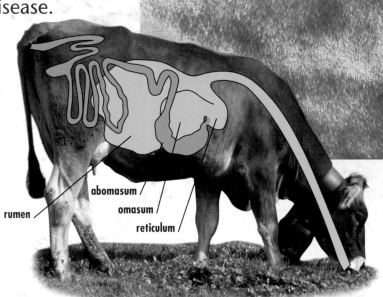

◄ This LM shows the protist *Trichonympha*, 200µm long, using its many beating flagella to move inside a termite's gut. Magnification: **x500**

▲ The digestive system of cattle includes a large stomach with four chambers (in order): rumen, reticulum, omasum, abomasum.

◄ Worker termites enter and leave their nest as they forage for wood and other plant food for the rest of the colony, including soldier termites like the one in the centre of the photo. Magnification: **x8.5**

Chewing the cud

They may be much larger than termites, but cattle have similar digestive problems. They belong to a group of plant-eaters called ruminants that also includes sheep and giraffes. A ruminant's stomach consists of four compartments including a large rumen (hence the name 'ruminant') that provides a warm home for trillions of bacteria and protists. As a cow grazes, it eats cellulose-rich grass that is digested by microbes in the rumen. Part-digested food is then regurgitated back to the mouth as 'cud' which is chewed again before returning to the rumen. Digestion is completed in the omasum and intestines, where some of the helpful and nutrient-rich micro-organisms are also digested.

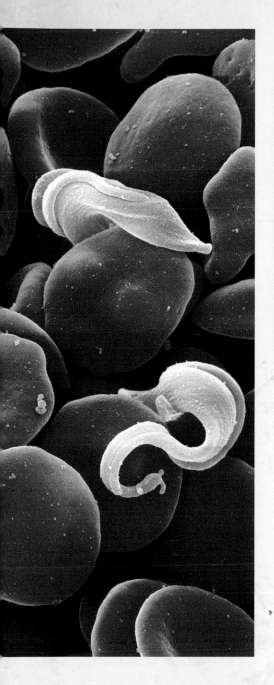

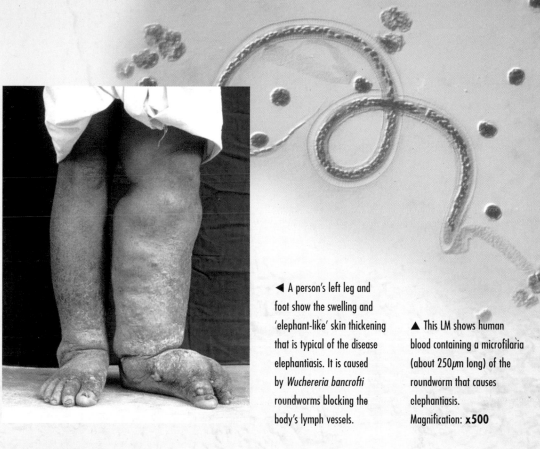

◄ A person's left leg and foot show the swelling and 'elephant-like' skin thickening that is typical of the disease elephantiasis. It is caused by *Wuchereria bancrofti* roundworms blocking the body's lymph vessels.

▲ This LM shows human blood containing a microfilaria (about 250μm long) of the roundworm that causes elephantiasis.
Magnification: **x500**

Intestinal upset

Not all pathogenic protists are injected by insects into the bloodstream. *Giardia lamblia* infects the small intestine, producing foul-smelling diarrhoea and excessive farting, a condition known as giardiasis. People pick up the parasite by drinking water or eating food contaminated with *Giardia* cysts passed out in other people's or animals' faeces. *Giardia* was first seen in 1681 by the microscopist Antony van Leeuwenhoek. During a nasty bout of diarrhoea, he looked at a sample of his own faeces under the microscope and found it to be swarming with the tiny pear-shaped creatures.

Worm threat

The tropical disease elephantiasis is also spread by mosquitoes, but caused by roundworms not protists. It affects 100 million people in South America, central Africa and Asia, and causes severe swelling of the limbs. As it feeds, an infected mosquito injects tiny microfilariae (larvae) of the roundworm *Wuchereria bancrofti* into a person's bloodstream. The microfilariae enter lymphatic vessels, a network of tubes that drains fluid from the body's tissues back into the bloodstream. Here they grow into larger adult worms that block the lymphatic vessels and so cause fluid to build up in the tissues, making them swell dramatically.

► This SEM shows protist parasite *Giardia lamblia* inside the small intestine (red). Around 10μm long, *Giardia* uses a sucking disc (darker green) to attach itself to the intestine wall.
Magnification: **x2,100**

Life on humans

From birth our bodies are home to many different types of bacteria and fungi. These micro-organisms occupy the body's outer surfaces (skin and eyes) and inner surfaces including the nose, mouth and the large intestine. A person normally carries about 1,000 trillion micro-organisms – ten times the number of their own body cells. Most are permanent residents that harmlessly co-exist with us, and even help us because they destroy pathogens that would cause disease. The body is also home to mini-animals including harmless eyelash mites, and harmful opportunists such as lice and itch mites.

▲ This handprint is made up of colonies of skin microbes. A hand was pressed onto agar gel leaving behind bacteria and fungi, which multiplied to form the colonies seen here.

Gut dwellers

Warm and moist, our colon (the longest section of the large intestine) contains more bacteria than any other body part. These trillions of mostly harmless bacteria help us in various ways. Colon bacteria protect us from infection by producing chemicals that deter or kill pathogens. They make B vitamins and vitamin K, essential nutrients that are absorbed into our blood. They also digest food our stomach cannot digest, a process that releases about 500ml of smelly gases (farts) daily. About 30 per cent of our faeces is bacteria (over 100 billion bacteria daily) hence the need to wash hands properly after visiting the toilet.

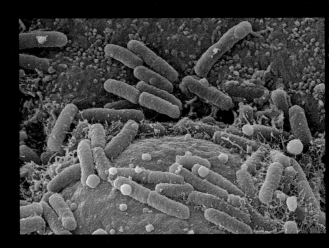

▲ This SEM shows the lining of the large intestine covered with rod-shaped *Escherichia coli* bacteria, each about 4μm long, one of the many types of bacteria in the human gut. *E. coli* is usually harmless. Magnification: **x3,060**

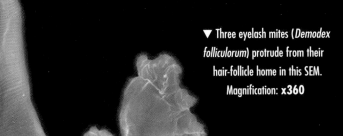

▼ Three eyelash mites (*Demodex folliculorum*) protrude from their hair-follicle home in this SEM. Magnification: **x360**

On the surface

Each square centimetre of our skin is covered by between 10,000 and one million microbes, depending on how moist the skin is (the more moist the better). But it is not easy for them to survive here. Salty sweat and germ-killing oily secretions kill many micro-organisms. Those bacteria and fungi that do settle are usually harmless. What is more, they form a community that stops harmful pathogens from living there, and so help to keep skin healthy. As well as microbes, all of us unknowingly have a population of eyelash mites. These tiny spider relatives, sausage-shaped and just 0.25mm long, squeeze into the follicles (pits in the skin) from which eyelashes grow. Here, they live harmlessly on a diet of dead skin cells and oily secretions.

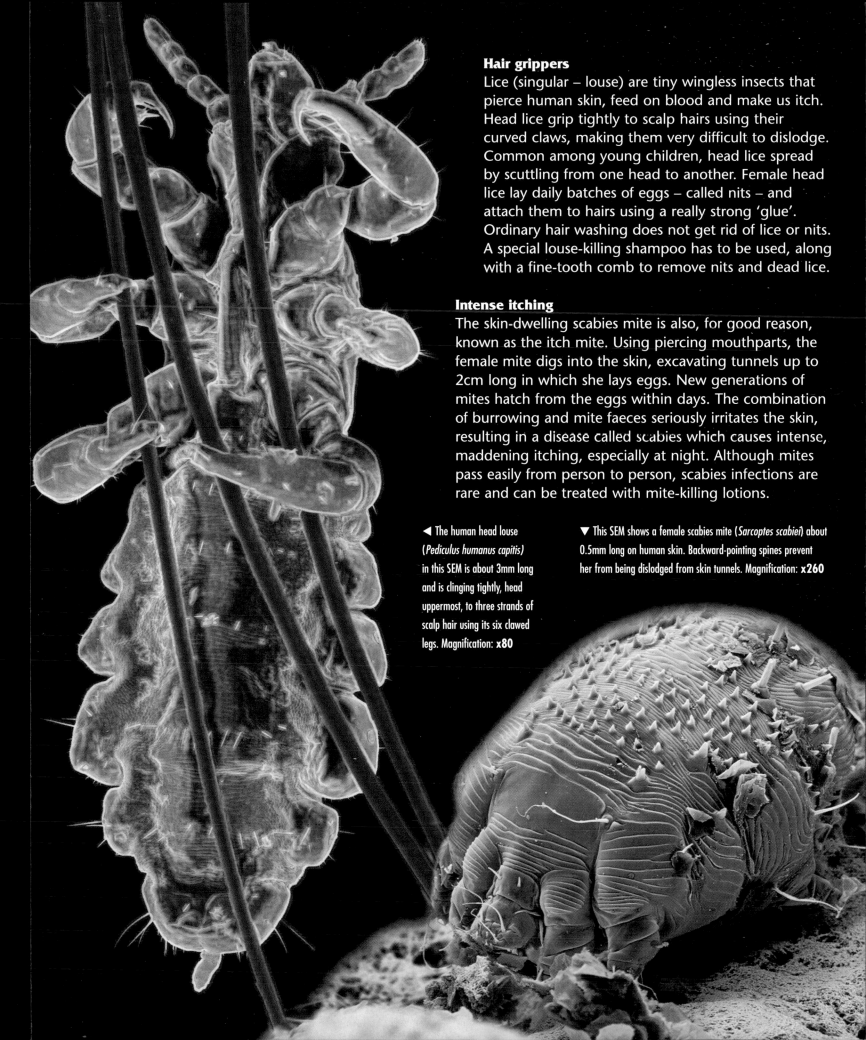

Hair grippers

Lice (singular – louse) are tiny wingless insects that pierce human skin, feed on blood and make us itch. Head lice grip tightly to scalp hairs using their curved claws, making them very difficult to dislodge. Common among young children, head lice spread by scuttling from one head to another. Female head lice lay daily batches of eggs – called nits – and attach them to hairs using a really strong 'glue'. Ordinary hair washing does not get rid of lice or nits. A special louse-killing shampoo has to be used, along with a fine-tooth comb to remove nits and dead lice.

Intense itching

The skin-dwelling scabies mite is also, for good reason, known as the itch mite. Using piercing mouthparts, the female mite digs into the skin, excavating tunnels up to 2cm long in which she lays eggs. New generations of mites hatch from the eggs within days. The combination of burrowing and mite faeces seriously irritates the skin, resulting in a disease called scabies which causes intense, maddening itching, especially at night. Although mites pass easily from person to person, scabies infections are rare and can be treated with mite-killing lotions.

◀ The human head louse (*Pediculus humanus capitis*) in this SEM is about 3mm long and is clinging tightly, head uppermost, to three strands of scalp hair using its six clawed legs. Magnification: **x80**

▼ This SEM shows a female scabies mite (*Sarcoptes scabiei*) about 0.5mm long on human skin. Backward-pointing spines prevent her from being dislodged from skin tunnels. Magnification: **x260**

Natural cycles

Living things are constructed from key elements, such as carbon and nitrogen. There is only a finite supply of these substances so, for life to continue, they must be returned or recycled to the environment when organisms die. Soil micro-organisms and mini-animals play a key role in recycling by rotting dead remains, releasing re-usable substances into the environment. The continuous exchange of substances between environment and organisms is called a cycle.

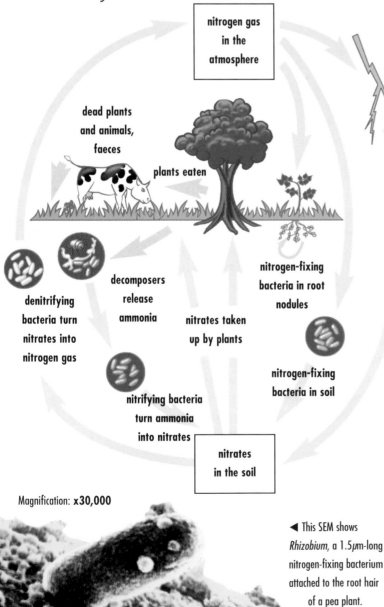

nitrogen gas in the atmosphere

lightning forms small amounts of nitrates

dead plants and animals, faeces

plants eaten

denitrifying bacteria turn nitrates into nitrogen gas

decomposers release ammonia

nitrates taken up by plants

nitrogen-fixing bacteria in root nodules

nitrogen-fixing bacteria in soil

nitrifying bacteria turn ammonia into nitrates

nitrates in the soil

Magnification: **x30,000**

◄ The nitrogen cycle — the grey arrows show how nitrogen moves continuously between living organisms and their non-living surroundings.

◄ This SEM shows *Rhizobium*, a 1.5µm-long nitrogen-fixing bacterium attached to the root hair of a pea plant.

Nitrogen cycle

Living things use nitrogen to make essential substances such as proteins and DNA. Plants take up nitrogen from soil in the form of nitrates and animals obtain their nitrogen by eating plants. Nitrates come from two main sources – nitrogen-fixers and decomposers. Nitrogen-fixing bacteria 'fix' nitrogen gas in the air, combining it with oxygen to make nitrates. Some exist freely in soil, while others live in plant root swellings called nodules. Decomposing fungi and bacteria break down dead animals and plants to release nitrogen-containing ammonia. This is converted into nitrates by nitrifying bacteria. The cycle is completed by denitrifying bacteria releasing nitrogen gas from soil nitrates back into the air.

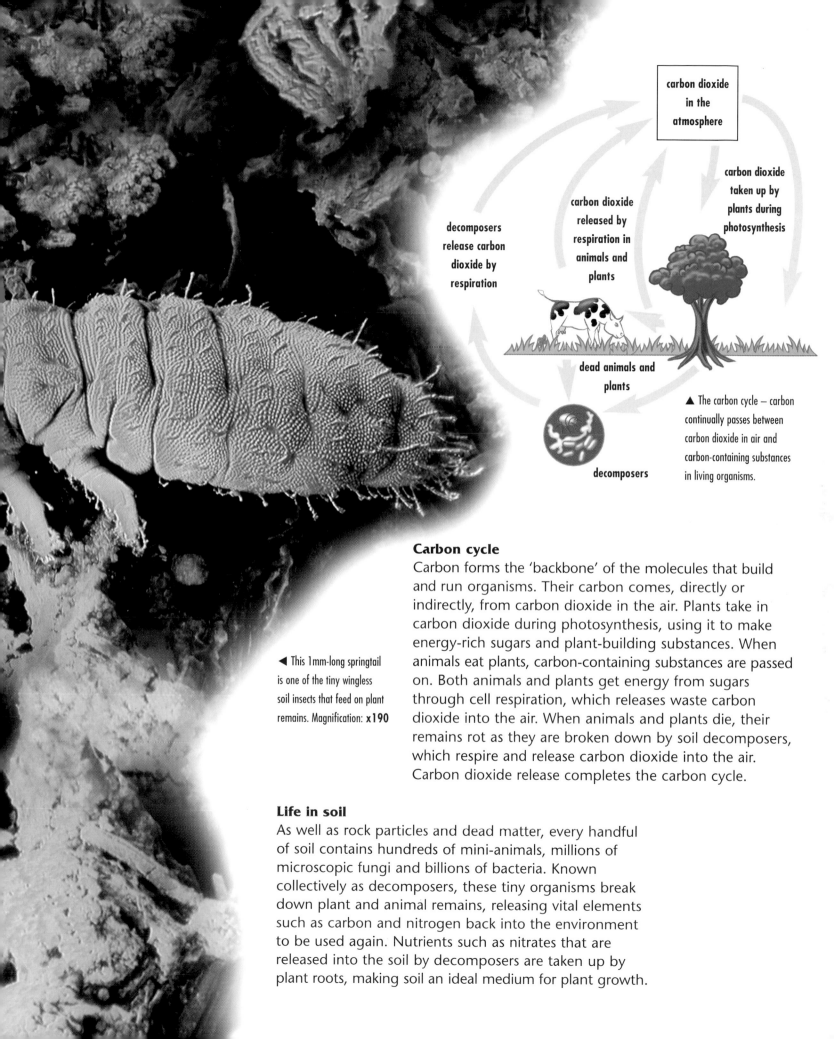

carbon dioxide in the atmosphere

decomposers release carbon dioxide by respiration

carbon dioxide released by respiration in animals and plants

carbon dioxide taken up by plants during photosynthesis

dead animals and plants

decomposers

▲ The carbon cycle — carbon continually passes between carbon dioxide in air and carbon-containing substances in living organisms.

◀ This 1mm-long springtail is one of the tiny wingless soil insects that feed on plant remains. Magnification: **x190**

Carbon cycle

Carbon forms the 'backbone' of the molecules that build and run organisms. Their carbon comes, directly or indirectly, from carbon dioxide in the air. Plants take in carbon dioxide during photosynthesis, using it to make energy-rich sugars and plant-building substances. When animals eat plants, carbon-containing substances are passed on. Both animals and plants get energy from sugars through cell respiration, which releases waste carbon dioxide into the air. When animals and plants die, their remains rot as they are broken down by soil decomposers, which respire and release carbon dioxide into the air. Carbon dioxide release completes the carbon cycle.

Life in soil

As well as rock particles and dead matter, every handful of soil contains hundreds of mini-animals, millions of microscopic fungi and billions of bacteria. Known collectively as decomposers, these tiny organisms break down plant and animal remains, releasing vital elements such as carbon and nitrogen back into the environment to be used again. Nutrients such as nitrates that are released into the soil by decomposers are taken up by plant roots, making soil an ideal medium for plant growth.

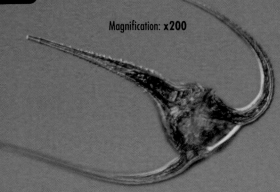

Magnification: **x200**

◄ This LM shows *Ceratium*, a 300μm-long dinoflagellate found in marine phytoplankton. *Ceratium* has long spines that help it to float, and flagella that move it towards sunlight.

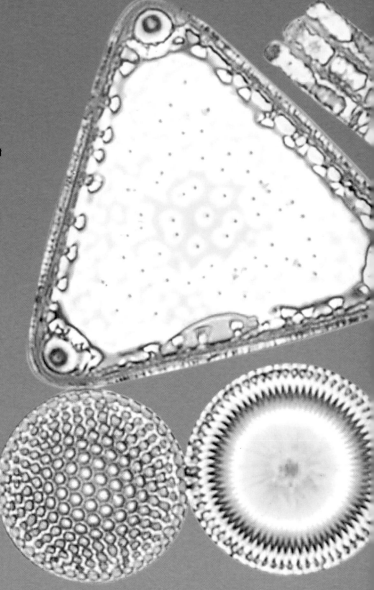

Ocean life

Oceans cover 70 per cent of the earth's surface. All living things in the oceans depend on plankton, the trillions of micro-organisms that float near the surface. Plankton includes both plant-like phytoplankton and zooplankton (protozoa and mini-animals). The name plankton means 'wandering' – many planktonic creatures can swim but are so tiny that they are swept along by ocean currents.

Phytoplankton

Phytoplankton contains chlorophyll and other pigments that 'trap' sunlight and use it to make food by photosynthesis. Phytoplankton includes algae (plant-like protists), such as dinoflagellates, as well as cyanobacteria. Importantly, these organisms provide food for zooplankton and so for all other ocean creatures. They also release oxygen into the air.

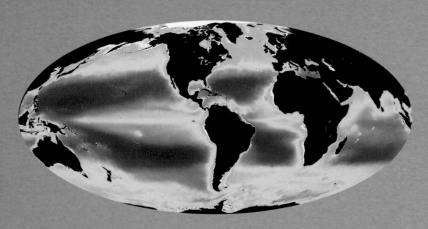

▲ This satellite photograph from NASA's SeaWiFS (Sea-viewing Wide Field-of-view Sensor) Project uses colours to show the distribution of phytoplankton in the oceans. Red areas have the most phytoplankton, through orange, yellow, green and light blue to dark blue with the least phytoplankton.

Uneven distribution

Phytoplankton is not spread evenly across the oceans, but thrives where seawater contains high levels of nutrients, such as nitrogen. These high levels occur in cold waters as currents bring nutrient-rich water from the depths where dead creatures decay and are recycled. They also occur where rivers wash nutrients into the sea. Amounts of phytoplankton are much lower in tropical oceans, where little mixing occurs between surface and deeper water.

Zooplankton

Ocean zooplankton contains types of most sea creatures. Some, such as copepods, spend their lives floating in the plankton. Others, such as the larvae of jellyfish, echinoderms (sea-urchins and starfish), crustaceans and fish, live in the plankton when young, but leave as they develop into adults. Zooplankton also contains protozoa, including radiolarians and foraminiferans that have delicate skeletons made of, respectively, silica and calcium carbonate.

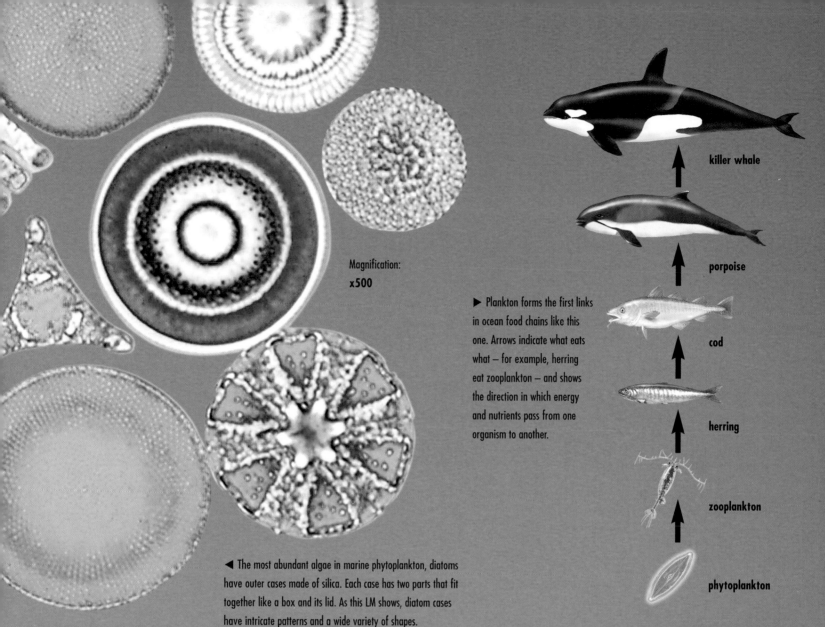

Magnification:
x500

▶ Plankton forms the first links in ocean food chains like this one. Arrows indicate what eats what — for example, herring eat zooplankton — and shows the direction in which energy and nutrients pass from one organism to another.

killer whale

porpoise

cod

herring

zooplankton

phytoplankton

◀ The most abundant algae in marine phytoplankton, diatoms have outer cases made of silica. Each case has two parts that fit together like a box and its lid. As this LM shows, diatom cases have intricate patterns and a wide variety of shapes.

Ocean food chains

A food chain links up to six species in a particular habitat according to what they eat and what eats them. At its base is a producer – a plant or plant-like organism that uses sunlight to trap energy which passes to species higher up the chain. Phytoplankton is the producer in oceans. In the example of an ocean food chain (above right) phytoplankton is eaten by zooplankton that, in turn, is eaten by herring, cod, porpoises and killer whales.

Ancient remains

When plankton die, any hard parts, such as skeletons or shells, sink to the seabed. Over millions of years, these tiny remains accumulate to form a thick layer that eventually turns into rocks. Calcium carbonate from foraminiferan shells forms limestone and chalk, exposed as white cliffs where land meets the sea. Glass-like silica shells from diatoms and other protists form the rock diatomite, which has many uses, including as a mild abrasive in toothpaste.

▶ Seen under a light microscope, this sample taken from the ocean's surface reveals some of the minute creatures that make up marine zooplankton. Easily visible here are circular, tentacled medusae — the larvae of jellyfish and their relatives. Darting between them, using their long antennae, are tiny crustaceans including copepods. Making up the mixture are the young stages of other types of animals. Magnification: **x30**

Living at extremes

We feel uncomfortable if summer temperatures hit 40°C, but how would we cope if they reached 80°C? Being that hot would certainly kill us and most other living things. So would being put in a freezer, exposed to radiation, bathed in acid, baked by the desert sun or being entombed in rocks. Yet there are certain bacteria that not only survive but actually thrive under such impossibly harsh conditions. Together, these resilient organisms are known as extremophiles ('lovers of extremes').

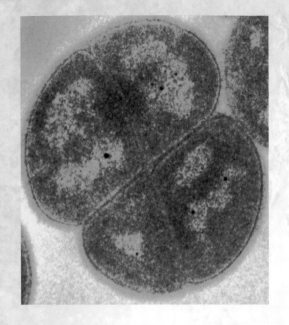

▲ The world's toughest bacterium, *Deinococcus radiodurans*, is not only unusually resistant to extreme heat, cold and drought, but also to deadly radiation. This TEM shows *D. radiodurans* arranged as a tetrad (four linked cells), each cell being about 2.5μm across. Magnification: x15,600

Extremophiles

In Yellowstone National Park, USA, the scalding-hot springs that bubble up through the earth's crust seem too hot for any life forms. Yet thermophilic ('heat-loving') bacteria that can tolerate temperatures of 85°C or more thrive here. Some even live in hot water that is acidic enough to dissolve metal. In the ocean depths, the thermophilic bacteria that live near vents which pour super-heated water onto the seabed include record-breaking *Pyrolobus fumarii*, a survivor at an incredible 113°C. Halophilic (salt-loving) microbes live in salt lakes, such as the Dead Sea, where nothing else can tolerate the saltiness. Cryophilic (cold-loving) bacteria get by in Antarctica at temperatures as low as -60°C. Other bacteria eke out an existence in solid rocks 3km below the earth's surface.

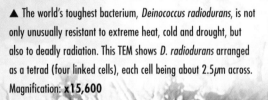

◄ Clouds of steam rise from the Grand Prismatic Spring in Yellowstone National Park. The rings of yellow and green are formed by different types of bacteria that thrive despite the high temperatures.

Radiation resistant

The most extreme of all extremophiles must be the bacterium *Deinococcus radiodurans*. Its name, meaning 'strange berry that withstands radiation', reveals its unusual ability. Radiation consists of high-energy alpha, beta and gamma rays, given off by radioactive substances, that can damage living things. *D. radiodurans* can survive exposure to over 3,000 times the radiation it would take to kill a person. It is also resistant to extreme heat, bitter cold, cell-damaging chemicals and dehydration. Research is under way to see if this supermicrobe can be used to convert lethal radioactive waste into something less harmful.

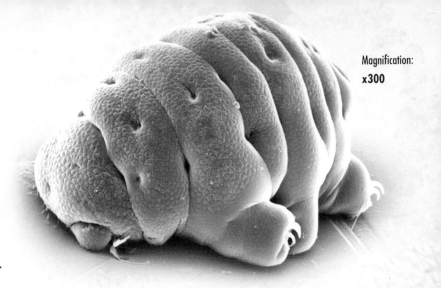

Magnification: x300

Suspended animation

Most bacteria are not extremophiles, but many survive tough times by going into suspended animation. They form apparently lifeless spores, called endospores, each surrounded by a thick wall that can resist extremes of heat, cold, acidity or toxic chemicals. Endospores can last for days, decades or millions of years. If conditions become hospitable, the endospore splits open and the bacterium returns to life. Mini-animals called tardigrades use a similar strategy. Wet-loving tardigrades survive dry periods by pulling in their eight stumpy legs, drying out, shutting down their metabolism and secreting a protective coat around their shrunken bodies. They can stay in this state for years, swelling up and returning to life once wet conditions return.

▲ This SEM shows *Macrobiotus richtersii*, a 300μm-long tardigrade. Also called water bears, these mini-animals live in damp and wet places, but can go into suspended animation if their habitat dries up.

Space survivors?

In space it is bitterly cold, without air or oxygen, and there is constant exposure to lethal gamma and other cosmic rays. But astrobiologists (scientists who search for life on other planets) reason that if life can survive harsh conditions on earth, then why not in space? Some argue that meteorites or comets could carry bacterial endospores. Or that *D. radiodurans* evolved on Mars then travelled to earth through space. Or even that life first arrived on earth billions of years ago on microbe-laden rocks from other planets. Science fiction or science fact? One day we may find the answer.

► In space, conditions are unbelievably tough. But some scientists have suggested that bacteria could survive there and that they may even have arrived on earth from other planets.

SUMMARY OF CHAPTER 3: INSIDE THE MICROWORLD

Enemies or allies

Are micro-organisms our enemies or allies? They certainly affect us by causing killer diseases, such as plague, AIDS and malaria, and a host of less serious ailments from colds to athlete's foot. But science has revealed not only which microbe causes which disease, but also how the body defends itself, and how we can protect ourselves using vaccination and antibiotics. The seriousness of disease overshadows the fact that only a few microbes are harmful. Most are harmless and some are allies, for example helping us to make food and drugs.

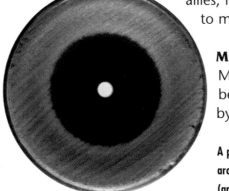

Microbes in nature

Micro-organisms also benefit all living things by playing key roles in the

A penicillin pellet (white) has a clear zone around it (black) showing where bacteria (green) have been killed by the antibiotic.

cycles of nature. When organisms die, for example, microbes recycle their remains, replenishing the finite supply of nutrients that living things need to survive. In the oceans, tiny plant-like plankton that trap sunlight energy are the food source for all marine life, at the same time releasing oxygen for us and other creatures to breathe in. Throughout nature, microbes form beneficial alliances with other organisms, so that both have an improved chance of survival. However, some relationships benefit one partner and harm the other, such as the parasitic protists and worms that infect humans and other animals.

Survive and thrive

We know that micro-organisms greatly outnumber us, existed on earth long before humans – perhaps arriving as earth's first inhabitants from space – and will continue to exist long after we have become extinct. Some even survive and thrive under extreme conditions of cold, heat and radiation that would kill the rest of us. As Louis Pasteur famously said when he acknowledged their superiority, 'It is microbes that will have the last word'.

Go further...

Learn a lot more about microbiology and microbiologists:
www.microbeworld.org/
htm/aboutmicro/abt_start.htm

See a cartoon of the discovery of the polio vaccine at: www.pbs.org/
wgbh/aso/ontheedge/polio/

For information about possible microbes in space go to:
http://quest.arc.nasa.gov/projects/
astrobiology/fieldwork/students.html

Read more about the *D. radiodurans*:
http://science.nasa.gov/newhome/
headlines/ast14dec99_1.htm

Microscopic Monsters by Nick Arnold (Scholastic, 2001)

Astrobiologist
Studies the possibility of life existing in space.

Biotechnologist
Studies the use of micro-organisms in industry, such as in drugs and food.

Environmental microbiologist
Investigates the use of microbes to remove pollutants from the environment.

Epidemiologist
Studies diseases and how they are transmitted through populations.

Immunologist
Studies the body's immune system and the use of vaccines to control infection.

See where penicillin was discovered: Alexander Fleming Laboratory Museum, St Mary's Hospital, Praed Street, London W2 1NY, UK
Telephone: +44 (0) 20 7886 6528
www.st-marys.nhs.uk/
about/fleming_museum.htm

Visit the MicroZoo at:
Armand-Frappier Museum,
531 Boulevard des Prairies,
Laval (Québec), Canada H7V 1B7
Telephone: +1 450 686-5641
www.musee-afrappier.qc.ca/
anglais/MicroZoo.htm

For more about immunology, visit:
Thinktank, Millennium Point, Curzon Street, Birmingham, B4 7XG, UK
www.thinktank.ac

multicellular
Describes an organism made up of many cells.

nitrogen
A gas found in the air.

nutrients
Substances needed by an organism to provide energy, and for normal growth and repair.

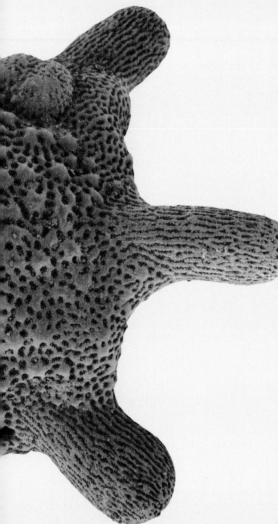

organism
Any living thing.

oxygen
A gas in the air that is used by organisms to release energy during cell respiration.

parasite
An organism that lives on or in, and feeds on, another organism.

pathogen
A microbe that causes disease. Also called a germ.

phagocyte
A general name for a white blood cell that engulfs and digests pathogenic microbes.

photosynthesis
The process in plants, algae and cyanobacteria that uses sunlight energy to make food from carbon dioxide and water.

pigment
A substance that gives an organism its colour.

plankton
The mass of microscopic organisms that drift in the surface waters of seas and lakes.

protein
One of a group of substances that perform many roles in all organisms, including construction.

radiation
High energy rays or particles that can damage living organisms.

reproduce
To multiply, or produce offspring.

RNA (ribonucleic acid)
The chemical found in certain viruses that carries instructions needed to build new viruses.

SEM (scanning electron micrograph)
A photograph taken using a scanning electron microscope.

silica
A glass-like substance that forms the shells of certain protists, and is also found in sand.

spontaneous
Describes something that happens suddenly without any obvious cause.

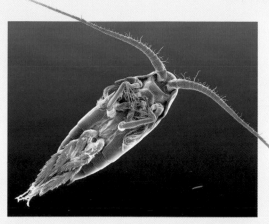

SEM of a marine copepod Magnification: **x14**

spores
Minute packages of cells that enable fungi to reproduce and spread.

stagnant
Describes water that is still, contains rotting matter and smells.

strain
A special type of a particular species of organism.

TEM (transmission electron micrograph)
A photograph taken using a transmission electron microscope.

toxin
A substance produced by certain pathogens which damages the organism that they infect.

trillion
A number equal to one million million (1,000,000,000,000).

tropical
Relating to hot regions near the Equator.

unicellular
Describes an organism made up of one cell.

vaccination
An injection of a killed or weakened pathogen or toxin to give protection against a disease.

vegetable protein
Food manufactured from a protein-rich plant source, such as soya beans.

Index

Acknowledgements

The publisher would like to thank the following for permission to reproduce their material.
Every care has been taken to trace copyright holders. However, if there have been unintentional
omissions or failure to trace copyright holders, we apologize and will, if informed, endeavour
to make corrections in any future edition.

Key: *b* = bottom, *c* = centre, *l* = left, *r* = right, *t* = top

Cover Volker Steger/Christian Bardele/Science Photo Library (SPL); 2–3 Lepus/SPL; 4–5*b* Eye of Science/SPL; 7*t* Lepus/SPL; 8*bl* R. Maisonneuve, Publiphoto Diffusion/SPL; 8–9*tc* Dr Gary Gaugler/SPL; 8–9*c* Sinclair Stammers/SPL; 9*tr* Biophoto Associates/SPL; 9*br* Andrew Syred/SPL; 10*cl* BSIP, Cavallini James/SPL; 10*c* Dr Gary Gaugler/SPL; 10*cr* SPL; 11*tr* K.H. Kjeldsen/SPL; 11*cl* Biophoto Associates/SPL; 11*c* © Dennis Kunkel Microscopy, Inc.; 11*cr* Robert Harding; 12*bl* Dr Jeremy Burgess/SPL; 13*cr* Michael Abbey; 14*bl* Dr Linda Stannard, UCT/SPL; 14–15*tc* Manfred Kage/Oxford Scientific Films (OSF); 14*br* A. B. Dowsett/SPL; 15*tr* © Dennis Kunkel Microscopy, Inc.; 15*br* Pascal Goetgheluck/SPL; 16*bl* Steve Hopkin/ardea.com; 17*tr* John Reader/SPL; 18*bl* Eric Grave/SPL; 19*cr* Eric Grave/SPL; 19*tr* Sinclair Stammers/SPL; 19*br* Francis Leroy, Biocosmos/SPL; 20*tl* Andrew Syred/SPL; 21*b* © Dennis Kunkel Microscopy, Inc.; 22*bl* Andrew Syred/SPL; 22*tl* BSIP, Cavallini James/SPL; 22*tr* Victor Habbick Visions/SPL; 22–23 *Background* Biozentrum, University of Basel/SPL; 25*br* Cristina Pedrazzini/SPL; 24*bl* © Dennis Kunkel Microscopy, Inc.; 25 *E .coli sequence of growth* Eye of Science/SPL; 26*tl* D. Phillips/SPL; 26–27*c* Biophoto Associates/SPL; 27*tr* © Dennis Kunkel Microscopy, Inc.; 27*br* Dr David Patterson/SPL; 28*bl* London Scientific Films/OSF; 28–29*c* Richard Packwood/OSF; 29*tr* Larry Michael/naturepl.com; 29*cl* Microfield Scientific Ltd/SPL; 30*tl* David M. Dennis/OSF; 30*bl* www.Micrographia.com; 30–31*b* © Dennis Kunkel Microscopy, Inc.; 31*tr* Kim Taylor/Bruce Coleman Collection; 31*br* Manfred Kage/Still Pictures; 32*tl* Dr Immo Rantala/SPL; 33*b* Andrew McClenaghan/SPL; 34*tl* Dr Jeremy Burgess/SPL; 34*bl* Lowell Georgia/SPL; 34*cl* Alfred Pasieka/SPL; 34–35*bc* Philippe Psaila/SPL; 35*tr* Richard T. Nowitz/Corbis; 35*cr* Russell Kightley/SPL; 35*br* NIBSC/SPL; 36*cl* David Scharf/SPL; 36*bl* Dr Tony Brain/SPL; 36–37*c* Bettmann/Corbis; 37*tr* © Dennis Kunkel Microscopy, Inc.; 37*br* Owen Franken/Corbis; 38*tl* Sami Sarkis/Alamy; 38*bl* Rex Features; 38*br* Biophoto Associates/SPL; 39*tl* Brian Hawkes/NHPA; 39*r* Holt Studios/Nigel Cattlin; 40*bl* Linda Steinmark, Custom medical stock photo, SPL; 40*br* Dr Steve Patterson/SPL; 40–41 Dr Tony Brain/SPL; 40*tr* A. B. Dowsett/SPL; 41*tc* Sinclair Stammers/SPL; 41*tr* SPL; 42*c* BSIP, Cavallini James/SPL; 42*bl* Bernard Pierre Wolff/SPL; 42–43*tc* The Art Archive; 43*br* Bettman/Corbis; 44*tl* Archives Charmat/Bridgeman Art Library; 44–45*bc* Corbis; 43*tl* Richard T. Nowitz/SPL; 45*tr* Wellcome Library, London; 46*bl* OSF; 50*bl* (*background*) Eric Grave/SPL; 46*c* Richard T. Nowitz/Corbis; 46–47*tc* Dr Kari Lounatmaa/SPL; 47*tr* Michael Fogden/OSF; 47*b* Georgette Douwma/SPL; 48*cl* CNRI/SPL; 48*br* Martin Dohrn/SPL; 48–49*t* SPL; 49*tr* Sinclair Stammers/SPL; 49*cl* R. Umesh Chandrian, TDR, WHO/SPL; 49*br* Lepus/SPL; 50*tl* Science Pictures Ltd./SPL; 50*bl* Eye of Science/SPL; 50*cr* SPL; 50*l* Garry Hunter for LAB/The Wellcome Trust; 50*br* Eye of Science/SPL; 52*bl* Dr Jeremy Burgess/SPL; 52–53*c* Dr Jeremy Burgess/SPL; 54*tl* Sinclair Stammers/SPL; 54*bl* provided by the SeaWiFS Project, NASA/Goddard Space Flight Center and ORBIMAGE; 54–55*tc* M. I. Walker/Wellcome Photo Library; 55*br* Douglas P. Wilson, Frank Lane Picture Agency/Corbis; 56*tl* Uniformed Services University of the Health Sciences, Bethesda, MD USA; 56*bl* Jim Brandenberg/Minden/FLPA; 57*tr* Microfield Scientific Ltd./SPL; 57*br* Dr Fred Espenak/SPL; 58*cl* John Durham/SPL; 59*br* © Dennis Kunkel Microscopy, Inc.; 60*bl* Dr Immo Rantala/SPL; 60–61*c* © Dennis Kunkel Microscopy, Inc.; 61*tr* © Dennis Kunkel Microscopy, Inc.; 64*br* © Dennis Kunkel Microscopy, Inc.

The publisher would like to thank the following illustrators:
Peter Clayman 50*c*; Sebastien Quigley (Linden Artists) 12–13,
16–17, 18*tl*, 18–19*c*, 22*bl*, 24–25, 27*cr*, 46*l*, 47*tr*;
Steve Weston (Linden Artists) 49*r*.

The author would like to thank Carron Brown for her diligence
and enthusiasm, Peter Clayman for his inspired designs, the
other members of the Kingfisher team for their hard work,
and Dr John Grainger for his pertinent comments.

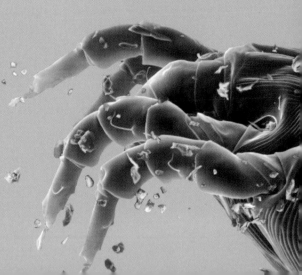

SEM of a dust mite
Magnification: x553